This
Jesus of Na
Without Money
Conquered More Millions Than
Alexander, Caesar, Mohammed, and Napoleon;
Without Science and Learning,
He Shed More Light on Things Human and Divine
Than All Philosophers and Scholars Combined;
Without the Eloquence of Schools,
He Spoke such Words of Life as
Were Never Spoken Before or Since,
And Produced Effects Which Lie Beyond
The Reach of Orator or Poet;
Without Writing a Single Line,
He Set More Pens in Motion,
And Furnished Themes for More Sermons,
Orations, Discussions, Learned Volumes,
Works of Art, and Songs of Praise
Than the Whole Army of Great Men
Of Ancient and Modern Times.

Philip Schaff, "*The Person of Christ*"
American Tract Society, 1913.

What Jesus Is Doing Through
Prayer Cookbook for Busy People™ Series

And John, calling two of his disciples to him, sent them to Jesus, saying, "Are you the coming One, or do we look for another?"

And that very hour He cured many of infirmities, afflictions, and evil spirits; and to many blind He gave sight.

Jesus answered and said to them, "Go and tell John the things you have seen and heard: that the blind see, the lame walk, the lepers are cleansed, the deaf hear, the dead are raised, the poor have the gospel preached to them. And blessed is he who is not offended because of Me."

Luke 7:19-23

> **"And they overcame him by the blood of the lamb
> and by the word of their testimonies . . ."**

Rev 12:11

"I must share with you and let the whole world know that God still answers prayer. The G5 Report Prayers has made a tremendous change in my health. Now I believe that all you need is just the right information about a problem and the right prayer bullets and you will access the heaven back door. My menstrual cycle seized due to Polycystic Ovarian Syndrome (PCOS) but I have being praying believing God. Using all your bullet and midnight prayers.

I decided not to believe the doctors report but to believe God who has the final report about my health. I refused to go for surgery. After the G5 Report prayers, I dreamt where I was menstruating in the dream. I used the Dream Code prayers to back it up. The next morning my menses started again normally. Not only was I healed, Man of God, but I was made whole. Thank you sir. May God do to all that will come across this G5 report as he has done to me."

Sister Hope, Nigeria

"In January 2007, I had a very evil dream. I dreamt that I had been bitten by a snake in the presence of my grandparents. I didn't understand what the dream meant and had not grown sufficiently in my spiritual life to deal with the dream as I should have but two weeks later, I became very sick. I was diagnosed with diabetes. Both my grandparents (on my mother's side—the ones in the dream) have diabetes. I went through a real furnace. Finally, after a period of feeling like the world has ended, I came across Elisha's prayer bullets. I prayed like I'd never prayed before, spent money on the gym, began to eat healthy, lost 10 kg, spoke the scriptures on divine health to myself everyday like a mad woman. Finally, in December 2007, I went for a medical exam. The results showed no trace of the disease. I'm totally free of diabetes. My grandfather was so encouraged by my miracle that he too started to exercise his Christian faith and he's now free of diabetes."

Deborah, Kenya

"I give this testimony to the glory of God. Since last year I have been praying one of your prayer points against attacks in the dream. My children used to go to clinic almost every month for fever and frequent stooling. One night in September in a dream a bird came and wanted to eat my child. I called Jesus (three times) and fire came down from heaven in the dream and burned the bird to ashes. Five days after this dream encounter, a big 'tree' fell in my family and since then my children have been enjoying divine health. To God be the Glory."

Samson, U.K.

"Praise be to God. I had a debt of $2,500 cleared in a way that was hard to believe. I saw it in a dream having cleared the debt but as time neared the deadline I kept trusting the Lord for a miracle. I later found out that the guy am doing business with had decided to clear the debt together with the interest. That is $4000! I asked him when he did that and he told me around the same time I saw it in my dreams. Praise the Lord."

Dionne, Kenya

"I was introduced to your site by a friend in January 2009. The spirit of death was over my head, but today I sing Hallelujah. I have three of your books. When I read or fire a prayer bullet, it shoots directly to the target. The spirit of death was vomited in my dreams a week after my 21 day fast. I prayed for fruit of the womb for a lady who could not conceive in four years. A month later she is pregnant. She is so happy for an instant answer. My husband is now back home. He used to work very far from home, but now he is back with promotion. Milk and honey is back into our marriage. My dream life is as clear as crystal glass. Praise the Lord."

Sibongile, South Africa

"I have a great news for you. I am so happy for what the Lord did in my life after praying with one of the prayer points you sent to me. It says 'Oh God send your angels to search the land of the dead and living and recover all my stolen blessings.'

I took a week off from work to pray this single prayer point. To my amazement four days after I started praying, by 1:00 a.m. a huge angel stood by me to take my certificate back which was devalued by a woman I gave it to for safe keeping 10 years ago. I was later told my certificate was kept in the waters spiritually.

Five days later I was called to complete an employment form in a company I have been working for as a contract staff for the past 10 years without conversion to a permanent staff. A week later I was called to collect my letter of employment as a permanent staff with 200 percent increase to my present salary in addition to so many benefits.

My God is good and He will bless you for what He has used you to accomplish in my life."

Nanre, Nigeria

"I want to share with you my good news that happened to me on Thursday 18th May. You know that I did that foundational prayer you sent . . . for 21 days with fasting and I stopped on the 9th of May. It has only been a week that I've got my miracle.

Do you remember me telling you about the vision of people giving me money and then this particular lady gave $1,000.00 but a big black bird came to snatch it away from my hand! But I went ahead to decree that the 'Angelic Executioner of God to execute the bird and also command the fire of God to burn it to ashes'.

Well just after finishing that prayer on the 9th . . . the next day I received $1,572.00 in check. And on Thursday . . . after work I went to the bank to withdraw some of my wages to buy our weekly groceries . . . guess how much was in my bank account! $8,000.00. At first I thought someone has put that money in the wrong account but we found out later it was definitely mine. I won't say where it came from but it is the work of our Almighty God. When I went home I received a letter from someone else saying that they have deposited $749.00 directly to my account. Our father is so faithful to his word.

Elisha since I've been using your materials I have been having miracles one after the other. Gone are the days of frustration and crying. Through your prayer points my relationship with the Lord Jesus has intensified so rapidly that I feel I am so close to him than before. The Holy Spirit has continually opened my eyes in the spirit and has been showing me greater things I've never seen before. I love him so much."

Sisilia, Australia

"Thank you so much for all the prayer points we've been getting the last three weeks, they have been awesome power packed prayers. I feel a calmness around me and I do not eat in my dreams anymore. Once I dreamt that I was on a podium and was preaching to thousands in an auditorium.

I received my financial breakthrough for my journey to the United States last week, waiting for the cheque to get clearance at the bank. I will leave Germany for the States next month by God's grace. Please I will need prayers on that. I need God's guidance. Thank God that I met you, I can feel a change in my life and my prayer life has gone up a notch."

Sister B., Germany

"All your books are Holy-Spirit inspired!! The Dream Code is so amazing!! The Prayer of Caleb is awesome.

I have learned so much from you. Such that, I don't even want to be prayed for anymore. When there is an alter call in my church, I no longer run to the front to be prayed for. I have learnt that I am justified by my words——speak the Word and engage in warfare!

In Africa where I am (South Africa), the enemy has a new strategy where young people (especially women) are lured to becoming traditional healers and these are professional people holding executive positions and/or working as 'consultants'. Now, when there is a conflict in the workplace——the directors would normally 'consult' these people for issues such as Change Management, Conflict Resolution etc. When these so-called 'professionals and/or consultants' come to consult, they bring incense ('impepho' in Zulu) and all their 'ingredients' and burn these things in the boardrooms. Nobody says anything because top management okays it (out of desperation for resolution in the workplace).

The enemy is really infiltrating the corporate world.

I believe it is time for a new army of the Lord to be raised who will know exactly how to 'neutralize' this epidemic and there is no other way than to learn to engage in warfare—aggressive prayers like you teach. May God bless you and your ministry!"

Juliet, S./Africa

"July this year I decided to tell my family members to take off three days to fast and pray for our family. None of them finished the three days but I did. I prayed at the midnight hour and I had this dream.

On the 3rd day of the fast, I dreamed me and my family members were in our home surrounded by water. Near our home, there is a big Indian sugar factory. I saw a huge monster come out of the factory and come inside our house. It would ask my father and mother for money saying that us and our neighbourhood were supposed to give it daily tribute. It would come both morning and evening daily and take our money.

Until I rose up, looked at it in the eyes and declared that it had no power over us, we belonged to Jesus and it should never again step in our house let alone take our money (my family had a problem of health. We would spend a lot of money, in fact almost all of it on every one's health issues—cardiac problem of my mum, my sister's breast masses, etc). I've noticed that this health issue is laying off slowly but surely."

Evelyn, Uganda

"Thank you Elisha for the great job you are doing. May God bless you abundantly. There was one of your prayer bullets that I used. It was about arrows of death. I prayed that prayer at midnight, and that night I had a dream. I saw myself inside a fridge buried underground. Thank God in that dream I had the power to get out. When I came out, I saw armed people coming to me. They were all carrying dangerous-looking weapons, but I told them that I serve the Living God. They came near as they wanted to finish me off but their weapons refused to work! Praise the LORD!"

Sister Faith, Ireland

"After studying your Dream Code, I felt like I received manna from heaven. The contents were an eye opener to me as far as dreams are concerned. When I started using the prayer points I felt a change in my prayer life. Thank you for teaching me how to deal with bad dreams/satanic attacks in dreams. I have now become a prayer warrior. I have also started spreading the message to other saints so they can experience the benefits of praying at the midnight hour."

Nancy, Zimbabwe

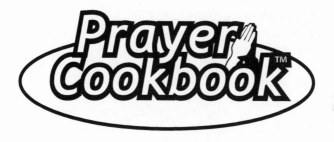

FOR BUSY PEOPLE

BOOK FOUR

CRACKING THE DREAM CODE

91 Dream Secrets Revealed, Plus 111 Prayers Bullets to Manifest Your Success Dreams— and Cancel the Bad and the Ugly!

With an Electrifying Story—of The Scientist Whose Dream Changed the World—In His Own Words!

BOOK FOUR

CRACKING THE *DREAM CODE*

ELISHA GOODMAN
Internet's #1 Prayer Coach
www.elishagoodman.org

If any of the readers of this manual want to receive hands-on coaching from me, send me your comments to my email: elisha.goodman5@gmail.com

Send your Praise Reports to: elisha@firesprings.com

Acts 2:17

"And in the last days," says the LORD, "I shall pour out my spirit upon all flesh, and your sons and your daughters will prophesy and your young men will see visions and your old men will dream dream . . ."

To all my online prayer eagles at **www.firesprings.com** who insisted that I create a realistic, simple and user-friendly manual to help them understand their dreams . . . **so they could take timely action.**

The Dream CODE

Contents

Introduction

Three Stories About Dreams

Cancelled the Dream Before It Happened

"*My name is John from Kenya. I work and live in Dubai and my wife lives in Kenya.*

On Saturday January 24, 2009, I had a nightmare, I saw a very big fire burning down a business and I was about 50 metres away coming towards the burning business.

Suddenly it turned that my wife was in the burning business and I could see ambulances rescuing people from the burning shop.

A person saw me and ran towards me stopping me from going near the fire and I noticed he was trying to stop me from seeing what was going on, since it seemed that one who looked like my wife was among the victims.

Then an ambulance from the scene passed next to me heading to hospital and I noticed my wife in it, badly burned.

I woke up in great fear and I heard a soft voice telling me to cancel that nightmare.

I said, 'Let satanic fire be put off by the blood of Jesus, I evacuate my wife from satanic fire in Jesus name . . .' and I continued as the Holy Spirit enabled me.

On 01-27-2009 I sent her some money which she was supposed to collect on 01-28-2009 in Nairobi. On Friday 01-30-2009, I called her to ask her whether she collected the money on 28th but she told me that she didn't go because she had strong force stopping her from going.

Then she mentioned about a supermarket which exploded in flames in Nairobi on the day she was to collect the money.

About 30 people perished in the fire and the bank my wife collects the money from is some hundred of metres from the supermarket.

She told me that everyday she goes to collect the money I send, she must go to the supermarket for some shopping and moreover the time it burned, coincided with the time she always go to collect the money.

All these she told me before I had told her of the nightmare I had.

I thank our Lord Jesus for revealing this scheme of the devil and thank Him for you Elisha for before I knew your website, I didnt know anything to do with dreams, their meaning and how to cancel them.

When she told me about the fire, I heard the same voice say 'remember the nightmare?'"

John, Dubai

Received Healing Scripture in the Dream

"I remember about two weeks ago when all the doctors had told us there was nothing else they could do for my mother (she had cancer), and that she should stop the chemotherapy she had started. My sisters and brothers started crying because all hope was gone out of them. I stood and declared that 'I refuse to sorrow in the name of Jesus' and continued to comfort them that only God who I believe in can handle this issue now and that His name was going to be glorified.

That night He gave me a Scripture in the dream and I saw myself telling all the people in her room who had lost all hope that 'The Word of God says in Ps.91:15—He shall call upon me and I will answer him, I will be with him in trouble; I will deliver him and honor him.' Following the dream I got that night, the following day she was out of that hospital. She was due for the chemo which she took successfully and she is now at home, no pain, only glorifying God.

Yesterday she went for more check-ups and the doctors found that the level of the sickness (please forgive me, the doctors language is kind of difficult to understand) had dropped from 600 (for doctors this was completely abnormal and one would be considered dead or the situation is irreversible) to 77 (am told the normal situation is 0). The doctors were in complete shock at the results. One of the doctors who had taken on her case at the beginning, was consulted yesterday again on phone and he expressed a great shock to find that she was still alive and walking by herself and very much smiling.

One of the doctors (a friend of ours) had even stopped calling on us because she knew anytime Mum would be pronounced dead. When we told her about the results she just screamed in amazement and said only God could have done it.

They are still wondering what we did to turn the situation around. The Word of God tells us 'My people perish for lack of knowledge.'

Last night I dreamt seeing my mother back in her car driving full of smiles and people were saying that she must be crazy in her situation and she replied and said she got healed.

Rosanne, Uganda

Advanced Warning in the Dream

"We were given letters that we might be affected by retrench-ment in our company a few days later I had a dream and I was on the list of those who were going to be retrenched, what amazed me was all the staff members who were retrenched were cancelled in a black pen, my name was also cancelled . . . but with a pen that had no ink . . . I could only see where the pen moved over my name . . . now this called for prayer bullets . . .

We stayed for a month without any trace of retrenchment, on the last Friday, August 28, 2009 we had a brief meeting just before we knocked off and we were told on Monday people will be retrenched . . . I went home . . . and by the midnight hour I took some prayer bullets that u had sent me entitled 'did u know that . . .?'

I prayed them fervently and aggressively until there was so much outpouring of the anointing of God that I could not contain . . .

Monday I came to work as usual, my boss started calling people one by one then when it was my turn he told me that he was going to retrench me, but instead he chooses to give me an opportunity ton open my own branch on the same company and be the managing director. He even told me he will give the support and the company car so that after I am established. Glory!

NB! Other people were retrenched and those who were not retrenched, the salaries were deducted, mine got deducted also and I was given a chance to also market the company and that would add as a commission over and above my salary (i.e., before I open my branch)."

Turner, Botswana

These are just some of many inspiring stories you will read about in this book that will show you that God can use your dreams to reveal advanced spiritual information to you. All you need to do is understand the messages you are getting and what action to take.

This book will also provide you common dreams, their interpretation and what action to take. All from a biblical perspective, and not pop psychology.

You will be able to claim the good ones, and cancel the bad and the ugly.

Chapter One

Big Bam Boom

*J*ust recently someone, who is not a Christian, came across this story in a book and wanted to know what I thought of it:

> "*Several years ago, I had a recurring dream. It always started with a big boom, like a loud gunshot. And then a voice telling me, 'You're not dead. You need to wake up. You need to drive the car.' What car? There was no car in the dream! Nevertheless, because the voice sounded so urgent, I would try to wake up anyway.*
>
> "*No matter how hard I struggled in the dream, I couldn't wake up. I did wake up out of the dream itself, but I could never find myself waking up within the dream. I had this dream several times over a period of about two weeks. Then finally one night while I had this dream, I woke up in the dream. And after that I stopped having the dream.*
>
> "*I had forgotten about it, but one evening a couple of weeks later, I was a passenger in a car driven by a friend. I heard a boom. It sounded like a loud gunshot.*
>
> "*I remembered the voice from the dream telling me, 'You're not dead. You need to wake up. You need to drive the car.' So I woke up and found the car was on fire. I found out later that a huge tire had come off a semi-truck on the other side of the highway and had smashed into our car. Both my friend and I had immediately been knocked out, but my friend's foot was still pressing the accelerator. We were headed toward a head-on collision with oncoming traffic. "I awakened from being knocked out and took over driving the car. I leaned over quickly, grabbed the steering wheel and turned the car to take it off the road. "If I hadn't had that dream, I'm certain both my friend and I would be dead*"

This is the sort of dream that mystifies, enthralls and fascinates us, especially those who do not know or understand what dreams are about.

This is an example of a dream warning. It tells of danger ahead.

The thing to do is:

Cancel it through prayers so it will not even have a chance to manifest in the physical.

Here's a simple prayer to deal with it:

> *"I cancel this bad dream in the name of Jesus and I declare that tragedy and calamity is not my lot according to the Word of God"*

That is for those who know JESUS as Lord and savior.

For others who may not have a relationship with the Lord Jesus, it is a wake-up call. Jesus loves you and wants to help you. But a relationship with Him is required before you can pray the type of prayer above and get result.

Because if you noticed, the prayer is in His name. The Bible declares that there is no other name given among men by which we may be saved.

When you've given your life to Jesus, and you want help and healing, there are prayers at the back of this manual. These are 111 targeted, precision prayers that can deal with every conceivable dream experience you may have. But before we get to it, there's a related information that is perhaps more important that I want to share with you on the very next page.

Chapter Two

The Scientist Whose Dream Changed the World

The physicist, Albert Einstein, is considered one of the greatest scientists who ever lived. Did you ever know that his big breakthrough *Theory of Relativity* came to him <u>in a dream</u>?

In her book, *"Wake Up to Your Dream"* Sandra Collier discussed how dreaming affected Albert Einstein.

Hear Einstein himself tell his dream

> *"I was sledding with my friends at night. I started to slide down the hill but my sled started going faster and faster. I was going so fast that I realized I was approaching the speed of light. I looked up at that point and I saw the stars. They were being refracted into colors I had never seen before. I was filled with a sense of awe. I understood in some way that I was looking at the most important meaning in my life."*
>
> *Years later, Einstein said, "I knew I had to understand that dream and you could say, and I would say, that my entire scientific career has been a meditation on my dream."*

Einstein realized that secrets had been revealed to him in the dream but he needed to understand what they meant. His dream helped him realize what lay before him. It laid the foundation for the greatest scientific advancement the world had ever known.

Chapter Three

I Have a Dream But I Don't Understand It

$\mathcal{D}$reams have been here as long as mankind.

Back in the Roman Era, striking and significant dreams were submitted to the Senate for analysis and interpretation.

In those days, dream interpreters accompanied military leaders into battle. Dreams were extremely significant and often seen as messages from the gods. People with particularly vivid and significant dreams were believed to be blessed and were considered special. People who had the power to interpret dreams were looked up to and seen as divinely gifted.

○ We know the Bible story of Joseph and how his divine ability to interpret dreams helped promote him from prison to prime minister in Egypt.

○ The story of Daniel is also familiar to many of us. His ability to interpret dreams catapulted him from slave-boy to first president in Babylon.

Dreams can carry vitally important information, sometimes delivered in coded form!

Gaining an understanding of your dreams can help you discover the hidden secrets of your life and how things may unfold in front of you. You may be given information that you may not have known otherwise.

To add to this, God can give you that special ability to interpret your dreams, just like HE gave to Joseph and Daniel in the Bible.

By asking God for the gift of dream interpretation, you will be in a position to unravel the true meaning of your dreams and understand their significance not only to you but also to those around you.

In order to understand dreams, you must be able to receive spiritual information from the Holy Spirit. That way, you will be able "discern" the meaning of symbols you see in the dream. Each symbol has a meaning, whether hidden or direct.

Such symbols can tell you:

○ If prosperity is coming your way and how to position yourself to receive it

○ If there's a warning you should not ignore

○ How a change of behavior or attitude can impact your relationships for either good or bad

○ If God is trying to get your attention

And so much more!

Many dreams are prophetic. They carry signs of warning and advice.

As you read through the following pages, you'll discover that every detail, even the minutest element in your dream may be important and should be considered when analyzing your dreams.

Once you know the meaning of your dreams, you'll be able to untangle the mystery of your foundation as well. You will even be given prayers that have been known to help those who had troubled dreams.

The first series of dreams will be about greatness, prosperity, abundance, wealth, and great relationships.

You'll see real life examples of famous people and how their dreams opened the door to success, peace, and prosperity.

5

Chapter Four

Dreams of the Rich and Famous

*I*n this chapter you will learn of famous people who became very successful through their dreams.

Jack Niklaus
World Champion Golfer

Dreams have been known to help people solve scientific problems, paint a masterpiece, or improve at sports.

World champion golfer Jack Niklaus told a reporter in 1964 that he used dreams to achieve championship success.

> *"Last Wednesday night I had a dream, and it was about my golf swing. I was hitting them pretty good in the dream, and all at once I realized I wasn't holding the club the way I've actually been holding it lately.*
>
> *I've actually been having trouble collapsing my right arm, taking the club head away from the ball, but I was doing it perfectly in my sleep.*
>
> *So when I came to the course yesterday morning, I tried it in the way I did in my dream and it worked.*
>
> *I shot a 68 yesterday and a 65 today and believe me it's a lot more fun this way. I feel kind of foolish admitting it but it really happened in my dream. All I had to do was change my grip just a little."*

Jack had a dream that skyrocketed him to success, fame and fortune.

Who knows, maybe you had the same kind of dream lately yourself.

Francis of Assisi
Catholic Saint / Founder—Franciscan Monks
Dreams played an important part in the life of St. Francis of Assisi. They gave him the strength to persevere despite his life of poverty, and helped him to establish his order of Franciscan Monks.

Just before a difficult interview with Pope Innocent III, Francis dreamt he saw a tall tree with thick branches.

The nature-loving saint looked upon it with wonder and realized that as he looked he grew in size until he was the same height as the tree.

When he touched its branches the tree bowed in reference.

7

While pondering this dream, Francis realized that this was God's way of telling him that he was blessed with favor before the Pope, and therefore the Pope would accept Francis' opinion concerning a crucial matter. He did.

Saint Francis had a dream that brought him favor, recognition and respect. What about you?

Adolf Hitler
Nazi Dictator
During the WWI, 28-year-old Adolf Hitler was a corporal in the German infantry, fighting in the trenches on the French Front.

One night he had a dream that he was being buried beneath an avalanche of earth and molten iron. He could even feel the terrible pain of being fatally wounded. He woke up and felt compelled to leave the trench immediately. As soon as he was clear of the dugout he heard a loud explosion behind him. The trench, where he was sleeping at moments ago, was now a smoldering pile of dirt, hot metal and blood.

This event convinced Hitler he was invincible and destined for greatness. The dream helped save Hitler's life for the time being.

(By the way, millions of people around the world would wish he never had that dream!)

The next time you have a dream of impending doom or danger, you will do well to take heed, because your prompt action may just save your life.

Oliver Cromwell
Founder of the English Parliament
When he was a young man Oliver Cromwell dreamt that a huge female figure drew back the curtain around his bed and told him one day he would be the greatest man in England.

The dream puzzled him because the greatest man in England at the time was the king. Cromwell remembered in his dream that there was no mention of the present king, only him being the greatest man in the country.

In 1648 after a bloody civil war, the king was disgraced and Cromwell quite suddenly became the greatest man in England. Oliver's dream prepared him for the pivotal role he subsequently played in the most powerful nation in the world at that time.

Charles Dickens
Famous Novelist
One night Charles Dickens had a dream he saw a woman in a red shawl with her back toward him.

"I am Miss Napier," she said as she spun around.

The dream didn't mean anything to Charles at first. But the next night after giving a literary reading some friends came backstage and introduced him to a woman they wanted him to meet. And you know what? Her name was Miss Napier.

Charles' dream helped him find love, peace, and contentment. He finally experienced joy in his life.

Elias Howe
Inventor of the Sewing Machine
Even the sewing machine owes its invention to a dream.

Elias Howe worked as a sewing operator and wanted to find a way to make his work easier. One night he dreamt that a savage king ordered him to invent a sewing machine.

After trying unsuccessfully, the tribe threatened to kill him with spears.

Just before they attempted to spear him, he noticed that each spear had a hole in it just above the point. This was the clue he needed to make the sewing machine a reality.

Elias's dream helped him solve a big problem he had and gave birth to the sewing machine.

Niels Bohr
Nobel Prize-Winning Physicist
Physicist Niels Bohr was trying to understand the nature of the atom. He tried several times to figure out the nature of the atom and how it was constructed. This problem perplexed him for a long time.

9

Finally, one night he had a dream. This dream showed the sun composed of burning gases with planets orbiting around it attached by fine threads. When he woke up, he realized that this was the solution to his problem.

He realized from his dream the structure of the atom, which heralded the birth of atomic physics. Bohr went on to win the Nobel Prize for Physics (the ultimate honor that any scientist can ever receive.) Bohr's son Aage also became a physicist and shared the Nobel Prize for Physics in 1975.

You may not be a scientist but everyday you are facing challenges in some aspect of your life, and may find the answer through your dreams.

Other Examples
Other notable examples of how dreams helped launch world famous careers include:

○ The great composer *Mozart*. He received many of his most glorious compositions through dreams.

○ The famous author **Robert Louis Stevenson.** He struggled to write a short story for days without much success until a dream showed him how to do it. The story he finished was the classic "Dr. Jekyll and Mr. Hyde."

○ *Dmitry Mendeleyev.* A brilliant 19th century chemist and physicist. He recreated the Periodic Table during his waking hours after it appeared to him in its entirety in a dream.

○ *Dr. Jonas Salk.* For years he treated people with polio. However, he was not successful due to lack of a vaccine to fight it. One night he had a dream that gave him the ingredients to make the vaccine. Because of that dream, he went on to create the polio vaccine.

The Sad Case of the President

A few days before he was killed, the famous American president, Abraham Lincoln, said that he was impressed that there were so many prophetic dreams in the Bible.

When his wife asked him why he'd brought this up, Lincoln related a dream he just had.

> *He was wandering through the halls of the White House trying to find out where the sound of weeping people was coming from. His search led him to the East Room where he saw a coffin lying on a platform, guarded by soldiers and surrounded by a throng of mourners.*
>
> *"Who died?" he asked.*
>
> *"The president. Killed by an assassin," was the answer.*

The sound of loud grieving sobs of mourners forced Abraham Lincoln to awaken from his dream.

Unfortunately for Lincoln, his dream proved real and it happened that a few days later he was assassinated.

Ignoring Your Dreams Can Open the Door to Disaster!

Chapter Five

Even the Bible Is Not Left Out

*a*s we've noted, dreams and their interpretation started many centuries ago. At least 28 of them are recorded in the Bible. We'll see the example of famous Bible dreamers and interpreters and how dreams brought them fame, recognition, and power.

Abraham

It was a dream that Abraham had that foretold his people's slavery in Egypt and their eventual Exodus.

> *"After a while the sun was about to set, and a deep sleep fell upon Abram, and, look! A frightfully great darkness was falling upon him. And he began to say to Abram: 'You may know for sure that your seed will become an alien resident in a land not theirs, and they will have to serve them, and these will certainly afflict them for four hundred years. But the nation that they will serve I am judging, and after that they will go out with many goods.'"*
>
> (Genesis 15:12-14)

Jacob

One of the earliest and most well known biblical dreams is Jacob's dream of a ladder from the earth to heaven. In the dream, God promised Jacob that all the families of the earth would be blessed through Abraham his grandfather. And that God would return Jacob to the Promised Land.

Joseph

Dreams caused untold hardship for Joseph.

> *"Look! Here comes the dreamer. And now come and let us kill him and throw him into one of the waterpits; and we must say a vicious wild beast devoured him. Then let us see what will become of his dreams."*
>
> *(Genesis 37:19)*

Joseph was thrown into a pit and eventually sold to traders, who brought him to Egypt. But Joseph's understanding of dreams got him recognition, blessings, and prosperity.

His interpretation of Pharaoh's dreams led to his appointment as Prime Minister of Egypt and saved his entire family from famine.

Daniel

As described in the book of Daniel, the dream that King Nebuchadnezzar of Babylon had a significant Biblical dream.

> *Nebuchadnezzar dreamt of a tree being cut down, and of being left to graze like a beast. Daniel explained that this dream was to teach him to acknowledge God above him in the same way as he was above the beasts in the field. Nebuchadnezzar eventually went insane, and his son Belshazzar assumed the throne. During a feast given by Belshazzar, Daniel saw a message of judgment in God's handwriting on the palace wall.*
>
> *The words he saw inscribed were ME'NE, ME'NE, TE'KEL, and PAR'SIN. Daniel proceeded to interpret those words to the king, "This is the interpretation of the word: ME'NE, God has numbered the days of your kingdom and has finished it. TE'KEL, you have been weighed in the balances and have been found deficient. PE'RES, your kingdom has been divided and given to the Medes and the Persians."*
>
> *(Daniel 5:25-28)*

That very night the Medo-Persian army captured Babylon and killed Balshazzar, and King Darius became ruler.

Modern Christians and Dreams

Early Christians taught that sometimes God reveals himself through dreams. However, in time dreams fell out of fashion within Christianity, thanks in part to Martin Luther, the great reformer, who did not want Christians to be carried away by dreams and their meanings.

In spite of this, it is clear that there are many references to God-inspired dreams in the Scriptures. In both Old and New Testaments, dreams and visions were regarded as revelations from God.

In fact dreams played a crucial role in the birth and life of our Lord JESUS Christ.

13

> While Joseph and Mary were first together an angel appeared to Joseph in a **dream** with this message: "Joseph, son of David, do not be afraid to take Mary your wife home, for that which has been begotten in her is by the Holy Spirit. She will give birth to a son, and you will call his name Jesus, for he will save his people from their sins."
>
> (Matt 1:20-21)

> The wise men after being guided by a star to the stable where Jesus was born were "given divine warning in a **dream** not to return to Herod . . ."
>
> (Matt 2:12)

Joseph is then warned in a **dream** to:

> "Get up, take the young child and its mother and flee into Egypt, and stay there until I give you word; for Herod is about to search for the young child to destroy it."
>
> *(Matt 2:13)*

Joseph remained in Egypt until he received these instructions from an angel in a **dream**:

> "Get up, take the young child and its mother and be on your way into the land of Israel, for those who were seeking the soul of the young child are dead."
>
> *(Matt 2:20)*

Thirty years later, while Pilate was contemplating the fate of Jesus, he receives this message from his wife:

> "Have nothing to do with that righteous man, for I have suffered a lot today in a **dream** because of him."
>
> *(Matt 27:19)*

As you can clearly see, some dreams are not just contrived by people, God can also have a hand in them.

CHAPTER SIX

DREAM INSTRUCTIONS

Some dreams can come from our thoughts and preoccupations during the day, while others can be direct revelations from God.

Here are some examples of what God Himself says about dreams:

> "And he went on to say: 'Hear my words, please. If there came to be a prophet of yours for God, it would be in a vision I would make myself known to him. In a dream I would speak to him.'"
>
> *(Numbers 12:6)*
>
> "And after that it must occur that I shall pour out my spirit on all flesh, and your sons and your daughters will certainly prophesy. As for your old men, dreams they will dream. As for your young men, visions they will see."
>
> *(Joel 2:28)*
>
> "The prophet with whom there is a dream, let him relate the dream; but the one with whom my own word is, let him speak forth my word truthfully."
>
> *(Jeremiah 23:28)*
>
> "For God speaks once, and twice—though one does not regard it—in a dream, a vision of the night, when deep sleep falls upon men, during slumbers upon the bed."
>
> *(Job 33:14, 15)*

As you see from the biblical references here, God does speak to people in dreams. Even today God can speak to you through dreams.

Dream Instructions

When we dream, sometimes what is told to us is in some form of instruction. This instruction can be from God, through His angels, or it could be our own minds, processing the data we received throughout the day, and any previous days. Or it could be from the devil.

The only problem is: Many modern Christians have no idea what to do with revelations that God gives through dreams.

There are many Scriptures in the Bible that can help us in this respect, if only we are diligent to study and apply them. If we only follow those Scriptures and understand what they say, we would realize that dreams are important part of our existence and can help us or save us at crucial moments of our lives.

The Bible even says that God will not do anything unless he first reveals it to some of his people, as Amos 3:7 states: "For the Sovereign Lord will not do a thing unless he has revealed his confidential matter to his servants the prophets."

God does reveal things to people—through, dreams, visions, etc. The only challenge is that most people just don't understand it.

Dreams can help warn us of impending doom. If we ignore it, our ignorance could cost us our lives.

For example, Paul, in the midst of a tempest and threat of a shipwreck told the people concerning a vision he had in the night. In it, an angel of God had appeared to him to assure him that no lives would be lost, even though everything pointed to the contrary. Paul regained strength and supernatural confidence from this visitation.

Besides giving you warnings, God can use dreams to reveal His plans for your life. A case in point is King Solomon.

King Solomon was the wisest and richest man who ever lived.

Here's the Bible account of what happened to him:

> "In Gibeon God appeared to Solomon in a dream by night; and God proceeded to say: 'Request what I should give you . . . For the reason that you have requested this thing and have not requested for yourself many days nor requested for yourself riches nor requested the soul of your enemies, and you have requested for yourself understanding to hear judicial cases, look! I shall certainly do according to your words. Look! I shall certainly give you a wise and understanding heart, so that one like you there has not happened to be before you, and after you there will not rise up one like you. And also what you have not requested I will give you, both riches and glory, so that there will not have happened to be any among the kings like you, all your days. And if you will walk in my ways by keeping my regulations and my commandments, just as David your father walked, I will also lengthen your days.' When Solomon awoke, why, here it has been a dream."
>
> *(1 Kings 3:5, 11-15)*

17

Chapter Seven

What to do with Bad Dreams

There's a class of dreams that bring anxiety, disappointment, depression and other types of emotions and moods.

Such dreams do not come from God. They come from the devil and his agents. Before we dive into this, let me quickly point out that there is yet another class of dreams.

This type comes as a result of what you are pre-occupied with in your day-to-day activities. And the Bible supports this view:

> "For a dream certainly comes in because of abundance of occupation, and the voice of a stupid one because of the abundance of words."
>
> *(Eccl 5:3)*

The Bible goes on to clarify:

> "Yes, it must occur just as when someone hungry dreams and here he is eating, and he actually awakes and his soul is empty; and just as when someone thirsty dreams and here he is drinking, and he actually awakes and here he is tired and his soul is dried out; thus it will occur with the crowd of all the nations that are waging war against Mount Zion."
>
> *(Isa 29:8)*

So it is important to point out here is that whatever your eyes and ears pick up during the day can be processed by your mind and projected into your dreams. That's why reading a dirty book or magazine, or even watching all these junk TV just before going to bed can lead to bad dreams. Because whatever pictures you present to your mind will be stored for processing and later retrieval.

That may be one of the reasons the Bible advises us:

> *"Therefore, since we have these promises, beloved ones, let us cleanse ourselves of every defilement of flesh and spirit, perfecting holiness in the fear of the Lord."*
>
> *(2 Cor 7:1)*

If you live a life as an alert and prayerful Christian, most of your dreams should be pleasant messages from God about your life and those around you.

However, just because we are Christians doesn't mean Satan will not attempt to infiltrate our lives through dreams.

In fact, the devil and his agents consider the dream realm to be a major theater of battle, where they launch all kinds of attacks against you, while you are asleep.

Jesus said that: **"While men slept, the enemy came and sowed tares."**

Satan has been known and will continue to project evil into the lives of millions while they are asleep.

Bad Dreams That Spell Trouble

Here's a good true-life example of dream manipulation. The story is told of a woman who was praying one night. Suddenly someone appeared to her and told her to stop praying. She was baffled when the person added, "You are praying too much." The woman paused and wondered why Jesus or an angel of God would ever ask her to stop praying when the Bible clearly says we should pray without ceasing.

So she looked closely and to her surprise, she noticed tiny dirty spots all over the white clothes of this strange visitor.

Immediately, a Scripture jumped into her mind:

> *"And no wonder, for Satan himself keeps transforming himself into an angle of light. It is therefore nothing great if his ministers also keep transforming themselves into ministers of righteousness. But their end shall be according to their works."*
>
> *(2 Cor 11:14-15)*

That opened her eyes. At once she yelled at him, "You . . . you cannot be a messenger from God. In the name of Jesus Christ I bind you now."

Just after she finished yelling those words, the person disappeared. The devil was trying to deceive her. He has deceived many through manipulations like this. He could even use the Scripture to try and get at us. That's what he tried with Jesus but it didn't work.

Satanic Attacks Through Dreams

Satan misleads millions every day through dreams. If you see accidents, attacks, closed doors, youth growing old, chains in the neck, closed Bibles, and other symbols, you are probably seeing the outworking of satanic attacks in the dream.

Everyone sleeps. God designed it so. Dreams are a part of sleep and play an active role in the lives of men and women. Everything God has designed for man is for a good purpose. The problem occurs when Satan and his demons are allowed to gain access and corrupt things. And this is what happens with many people. They have good dreams today, and the next minute the dreams have all turned to a nightmare.

Sometimes, people experience exactly what happened in their dreams the night or weeks after the dream occurred. For example, a woman dreamt about somebody who was polluting her head. Unfortunately, the church she attended did not teach her how to deal with such dream attacks, so she had no idea how to defend herself, nor did she know what the dream actually meant. Soon after the dream occurred, her husband started to turn against her and this eventually led to the collapse of her marriage.

A pastor once told a story of a newly wedded lady in England. She dreamt that a strange woman she'd never seen before walked into her home, made straight for her closet and grabbed her wedding gown. She was gone before you could say, "Jesus is Lord."

At breakfast the following morning, she told her husband about it. He just laughed it off. Tell you what? Exactly two months later, on the exact same day, her husband filed for divorce. The sad part of it was he packed up and moved in with—*you guessed it*—the strange woman who first appeared in the dream!

When people have strange or bad dreams, they should learn to cancel them through prayers so they can protect themselves from the harm the dream was designed to cause.

21

Chapter Eight

4 Spiritual Weapons for Dream Battles

*W*hen unchecked, Satan can use the dream world to his advantage. He has a very subtle strategy. What he does is that he allows two or three bad dreams to come to pass. When this happens you start believing that you will have bad dreams and those dreams will happen.

> *You must not allow the devil to deceive you. Instead, learn to make use of spiritual weapons freely available to all believers. Find out what those spiritual weapons are and use them.*

Of course, there are Christians who think they are protected and don't need the complete suit of armor from God (see Ephesians 6:11-13). They don't realize how Satan and his agents can manipulate the dream life of even the most mature Christians.

There are over a hundred spiritual weapons described in the Bible. You can use any combination of them in prayer to fight your dream battles. Please note that we are called soldiers of Christ. The work of a soldier is to fight. In our case, it is a spiritual battlefield, not visible to the naked eye, but real all the same.

Here I will just go ahead and describe four of these weapons. You can uncover the rest through a diligent study of your Bible.

○ **The Name of Jesus:** The most powerful weapon which is available for our use against satanic dreams is the use of the name of JESUS. The Bible says:

> *"The name of the LORD is a strong tower. Into it the righteous runs and is given protection."*
>
> *(Prov 18:10)*

No matter how terrible you are attacked in your dream, if you still have spiritual "fire" to call on the name of Jesus, no power will be able to overcome you.

○ **The Blood of Jesus:** The blood of Jesus is another weapon you can use against satanic dreams. This is clearly stated in the Bible:

> *"And they conquered him because of the blood of the Lamb and because of the word of their testimony, and they did not love their souls even in the face of death."*
>
> *(Rev. 12:11)*

○ **Fire of God:** The fire of God? What is this about? You may not realize this but the Bible does show that God is a consuming fire.

> *"For here God himself comes as a very fire, and his chariots are like a storm wind, in order to pay back his anger with sheer rage and his rebuke with flames of fire."*
>
> *(Isa. 66:15)*

○ **Angels of God:** Another weapon you have at your disposal are God's angels. Angels have always played a crucial part in battles for God through the centuries. They have also been used to protect his servants. The Scripture says this in Psalms 91:10-11:

> *"No calamity will befall you, and not even a plague will draw near to your tent. For he will give his own angels a command concerning you, to guard you in all your ways."*

Here's another in Psalms 35:4-6:

> *"May those be shamed and humiliated who are hunting for my soul. May those be turned back and be abashed who are scheming calamity for me. May they become like chaff before the wind, And let God's angel pursue them. Let their way become darkness and slippery and let the angel of the LORD pursue them."*

You must ALWAYS remember that angels are part of our weapons for spiritual warfare. Out of many.

As long as anyone decides to remain in ignorance she will not be able to withstand the arrows that are fired day and night. If you are facing attacks in the dream, remember this: You must put on the complete suit of armor from God, for without it you are vulnerable to attack and destruction.

Chapter Nine

91 Dream Secrets Revealed

*I*n this chapter, I will outline some of the dream symbols and their meanings so you will have the ability to recognize and understand your dreams and be able to take prompt and necessary action.

There is something I need to tell you at this point. A bad or negative dream is not an absolute. *It is a call to action.* No matter what the dream symbolizes, we have been equipped with the ability to turn the negative to positive.

With the right kind of prayer and action.

As soon as you wake up from a bad dream, you should cancel it. A simple prayer like this:

> *"I cancel that negative dream I just had about _____ (fill in the blanks) in the name of Jesus. I decree that it shall NOT manifest in the physical in Jesus' name. I release the fire of God on every satanic actor in that dream. I plead the blood of Jesus and I hold up the banner of victory in Christ Jesus. Let the angels of the LORD go on a "search and destroy" mission in the land of the living and of the dead . . . to destroy every power, spirit, personality, device, or animal programmed to attack me in the dream. Henceforth, let nothing trouble me in the dream for I bear on my body the marks of the Lord Jesus Christ. Amen"*

Now, a prayer like this goes very far. And very deep. In our Prayer Academy, I actually teach my students step-by-step what all this means.

I want you to note . . . as we take a sampler of common dreams . . . that we are approaching the subject of dream meanings from a purely biblical, spiritual perspective. That means, you are going to be hearing me use the word "spirit" a lot. You are going to see me identify the kind of spirits that are at play when you have certain dreams. And in many cases, the exact prayer point to use to neutralize their activities.

Let me drop a gentle note of warning here. The prayers for each of these dreams are not theory.

Like you see in psychology or New Age texts.

For example, many who have been going to the **wrong places** to look for the meaning of their dreams have been told that seeing snakes in the dream is positive, that it represents money or sustenance.

Nothing can be further from the truth!

You need to know that the snake or serpent represents the arch-enemy of God and man. And the Scripture is very clear what Christians should do with serpents. We are to *"trample upon them"* meaning stand against them and decree their destruction using the authority that our Lord gave us.

That is just one example.

As you read through the following pages, there may seem to be symbols or experiences you don't recognize or don't encounter in your dream life. That is OK. Take note of them anyway and compare notes with what you see in the future.

A Sample of Evil Dreams, What They Mean and How to Stand Against Them

1. **Car brakes don't work** means the enemy is trying to take control of a certain area in your life. Your destiny is under attack. You have to resist this using the Word of God and prayer. You should cancel the dream as soon as you wake up and pray that the heavenly mechanics would repair the brakes of your vehicle of destiny and ask the Holy Spirit to take charge in Jesus' name.

2. **Person who passed away takes something from you**
    means there is a spiritual link that you need to break. The
    enemy is using that link as a conduit to siphon your virtues
    and blessings. If the person is a relative, it means you have
    ancestral evil linkages to deal with. You can pray:

    > *"I recover my virtues from the land of the dead, and I cut every
    > ancestral evil linkage with the sword of the Lord in the name of
    > Jesus."*

3. **Being arrested** means you have fallen into the trap of the
    spirits which engineer bondage and captivity. You may be
    under a curse. You need to rise up with holy anger and pray
    like this:

    > *"I release myself from every satanic cage or prison in the name
    > of Jesus. I bind the arresters in the dream and I release the hor-
    > nets of the Lord against them. O Lord, dispatch your angels of
    > war to hunt down my captors and take my captivity captive in
    > the name of Jesus."*

4. **Wandering around in a bush** means the spirit of confusion
    is at work in your life. You will not be able to focus on any-
    thing and do it well. Confusion will be the order of the day.
    You need to bind the spirit of confusion. Ask the Lord to
    send his angelic dispatch riders to take you out of the maze
    of confusion.

5. **Bulls or cows chasing you** mean that witchcraft spirits
    are after you. Ungodly dream interpreters will tell you cows
    signify good times coming. That's a big lie. If you find cows
    coming after you in the dream, you better wake up and pray!
    Bind every spirit of witchcraft and release the fire of the Lord
    to burn them to ashes in Jesus' name. And learn to be sensi-
    tive to what's going on in your environment.

6. **Scorpion attacking you** means that you are up against very aggressive and wicked enemies. They will stop at nothing to destroy. Rise up and declare war against visible and invisible enemies. Pray like this:

> *"Thunder of God, scatter every satanic army assigned against my life in the name of Jesus."*

7. **Lost your clothes and not able to find them** before you woke up means spiritual robbers are working against you, and the end result is shame and demotion, unless you take action now. When you wake up, send the angels of God on assignment to recover what you've lost. Ask the Holy Spirit to arrest those responsible. Ask for the garment of honor and glory from the Lord.

8. **Walking around barefoot** means shame, demotion and hardship. Pray and destroy the powers assigned to monitor your life and report you back to your enemies. Bind the spirits of shame and poverty. Release the fire of God against them. Cover yourself with the blood of Jesus.

9. **Flood carrying your things away** means that evil consultants have been engaged to fight you. By evil consultants I mean psychics, mediums, fortune tellers, sorcerers, enchanters, magicians, etc. Their specific assignment is to destroy or transfer your virtues and replace them with trouble, tribulation and hardship. You will do well to learn how to battle against these things through violent prayer. A great prayer point to use is:

> *"O altar of perpetual destruction set up against me, be destroyed by the earthquake of the Almighty in the name of Jesus."*

You can also pray that the Lord should turn every evil counsel against you to foolishness.

10. **Seeing yourself flying** means you have been initiated into witchcraft, whether you know it or not, whether you agreed to it or not. Some people inherit this wicked spirit from their parents and have no idea that they are blind witches. The solution is to look for an anointed Christian ministry that understand how to set people free from this type of things. Five minutes prayers will not be enough to do a thorough job here. As Jesus said, *"this kind goeth not but by prayer and fasting."* It is a stubborn spirit.

11. **Being arraigned before a judge** means someone is placing curses on you. Here's where you need to know your Scripture. The Bible says, *"No one can curse whom the Lord has blessed."* And *"a curse causeless shall not come."* Armed with these Scriptures you pray:

> *"I cancel and nullify every curse placed upon me in the name of Jesus. I arrest every spirit assigned to enforce curses upon my life in the name of Jesus. I destroy their assignment by the power in the blood of Jesus. I declare that I am the blessed of the Lord. On one can curse whom the Lord has blessed."*

This is powerful stuff. And it works. And it is scriptural.

12. **Being driven to an unknown destination** means some other power outside the Holy Spirit is in control of your life, or an area of your life. For evil. Pray for the Holy Spirit to unseat the evil driver. Ask the Lord to forgive you where you have rebelled against Him, and opened the door for the enemy.

13. **Surrounded by bees** means you are under attack by strong, highly-organized enemies that will stop at nothing to destroy you. Release the fire of God to burn them to ashes, through aggressive and persistent prayer. That means pray against them every night until you see a sign of their defeat.

14. **Doors closing before you enter** means the spirit of Pisgah is after you. This is the spirit of "almost there." It makes people to fail at the edge of breakthroughs or miracles. It is a vagabond spirit. It led the children of Israel wandering in the wilderness for 40 straight years! You need all the spiritual ammunition you can gather against this one. More on weapons you need later.

15. **Seeing birds following you** means you are being monitored. Especially if it is a black bird. You are being observed and monitored for evil. You pray:

> *"Every evil observer, be roasted by the fire of God. In Jesus' name."*

If you are not familiar with what it means to be roasted, you need to take a reading tour of the book of Jeremiah. He used to pray that certain enemies should be roasted. Meaning the fire of God should burn them to ashes. Remember, the Bible says God is a consuming fire. See where that came from?

16. **Falling into a pit** means you are on a journey to spiritual slavery and captivity. Though you might be walking around in the physical free, if you see yourself in a pit in the dream, you have already been sold into slavery. And those responsible are those who are close to you. Maybe members of your family, either living or dead. Or workplace enemies posing as friends. Or even church members. Remember Joseph in the Bible. Remember the prophet Jeremiah. In both cases, it was envy and jealousy at work. They were both cast into the pit. You pray:

> *"O Lord, send your angelic hosts to rescue from the pit in the name of Jesus."*

Then you begin to declare like David in Psalm 40:2:

> *"HE brought me up also out of an horrible pit, out of the miry clay, and set my feet upon a rock and established my goings."*

17. **Being forced into marriage** means you have been married off in the spirit realm. You have a spirit spouse who will fight aggressively to ensure that you never get married in the physical . . . or if you ever manage to, that marriage will be hell on earth. This is how the stage is set for separation and divorce that is plaguing many today. Here's what you do: You rebuke those responsible for the marriage in the name of the Lord. Call on the fire of God to consume that evil marriage and release yourself from its consequences through the blood of Jesus. Declare that you are married to Jesus, and HE will not share you with another. After that, go into a period of extended fasting, praying Type 1 prayer points (i.e., foundational prayers . . . the kind we pray during our prayer marathons).

31

18. **Attending a meeting with unknown people** means you have spiritual linkages with occult and demonic groups. This kind of thing attracts the wrath of God very easily. Why? Any gathering that is not unto the Lord is a candidate for the destructive whirlwind of the Lord. You better not be around when it strikes. Pray and severe your link with unknown or known evil groups, and release the fire of God to scatter them unto desolation. For good measure, add this:

> *"I forbid any regrouping, or re-gathering of this group in the name of Jesus."*

19. **Going back to the old house** you lived in as a child means the spirits of powers of retardation operating in your family line is trying to cut short your progress and place a spiritual ceiling on your life. If you don't stand against this through prayer and fasting, you might soon find yourself

making negative or backward progress, being passed over for promotion at work, losing favor with friends and family, making silly mistakes that annoy your boss at work and can get you fired, etc. You pray:

> *"Every altar of backwardness in my fathers' house, collapse in the name of Jesus."*

Then you quickly follow up with this one:

> *"Let the habitation of humiliation and demotion be battered, shattered and swallowed up by the power of God, in Jesus' name."*

20. **Climbing a hill with difficulty** means serious obstacles have been placed on your path of progress. If you climbed the wall and when you stretch out your hand to get a good grip, it comes off, it means your faith is weak. You need to shore up your faith by studying the Word of God and prayers. Then you can declare like this:

> *"O Lord, let my trials become gateways to my promotions in the name of Jesus."*

21. **Teeth falling out** means there's trouble ahead. One that could take its toll on your life and that of your loved ones over a period of time, unless arrested. You can pray like this:

> *"Every power exploring devastating strategies against my destiny, receive the judgment of God in Jesus' name."*

22. **Lights going out** means a time of tribulation is just around the corner. This is advance warning. You gird up your spiritual loins and begin to pray like this:

> "O God arise, and attack my attackers in the name of Jesus. Let
> my problems expire, as darkness expires before the light in the
> mighty name of Jesus."

23. **Picking up coins** means you are under attack by the spirits
    of poverty. Please note that this is a stubborn generational
    spirit that is usually transferred from person to person, from
    one generation to another. You pray like this:

> "I bind the spirits of lack and poverty. I break the backbone
> of lack and scarcity in my life in the name of Jesus. Let the
> chapter of lack and want be closed forever in Jesus' mighty
> name."

33

24. **Playing on a losing team** means the Lord just released a
    significant breakthrough to you but before it could manifest
    in the physical, the enemy launched a strong counter-attack
    and stopped it from getting to you. Conversely, if you played
    on the winning team and your side scored or earned points,
    the miracle is sure to manifest with a few weeks, if you are
    prayerful and watchful.

25. **Strong winds blowing against you** means the spirits
    of sudden destruction have been unleashed against you.
    You have to stand your ground here, command every
    satanic wind to cease in the name of Jesus. Then you go
    on the offensive and unleash the whirlwind of the Lord
    described in Jeremiah 30:23. If you pray this particular
    prayer point at the midnight hour for just 15 minutes for
    a few days (see "Prayer Cookbook" on how to do this prop-
    erly) . . . within days, you'll be surprised at the dramatic
    turnaround in your life.

26. **Wild animals charging at you** represent raging and
    violent enemies. You begin to see problems coming at you
    from all directions. To overwhelm you and make you lose
    your sense of balance. To devastate you and keep you going

from one problem to another, in an endless loop. You have to pray like this:

> *"By the power of God, let every trouble in my life crumble, in the name of Jesus. Thou power of God, usher me out of the valley of tribulation by fire in the name of Jesus. Every power or spirit raging against me, collide with the Rock of Ages in the name of Jesus."*

When you learn to pray like this, don't be surprised when calamity suddenly overtakes people who have been conspiring against you secretly. Even though you are NOT praying against human beings.

27. **Seeing yourself being buried** means the spirit of death and hell is after you. Use the Scripture in Revelation 12:11 Then begin to pray like this:

> *"The anger of God shall write the obituary of all my oppressors in the name of Jesus."*

This is a midnight prayer.

28. **Shedding tears** means the spirit of depression and heaviness wants to afflict you. To make you sad and depressed. To make you mourn. The Scripture to use against this spirit is in Isaiah 61:3. Then you begin to pray:

> *"I refuse to mourn in the name of Jesus. The Lord shall give me joy and gladness and all sorrow shall flee away in Jesus' name. Amen"*

29. **Stagnant or dirty water**—Seeing stagnant water means your spiritual life is being polluted. Ask for the cleasing power of the blood of Jesus to wash you and remove every contamination from your life.

30. **Hair**—Losing your hair in the dream means a loss of glory
    and honor. If somebody cuts your hair in the dream, the
    enemy is sucking away your spiritual strength. And if you fail
    to take immediate action in the spirit, it will soon lead to
    other losses, disgrace and slavery. Remember Samson and
    how he was captured by his enemies. It began with the loss
    of his hair!

31. **Begging**—If you see yourself as a beggar or begging, the
    curse of poverty is on your life. You need to break that
    curse, destroy both the roots and the fruits in your life, and
    return arrows of poverty back to wherever they came from.
    Then use Scripture in Psalm 84:11 to ask for a release of
    good things and abundance into your life.

    35

32. **Traveling on an endless journey**—If you see yourself
    traveling on a journey that never ends, it means the spirits of
    the vagabond is on you. It's a hard road to travel, with dan-
    gers lurking on every side. You need to terminate that evil
    journey and command the fire of God upon all vagabond
    spirits assigned against you. You can read about how the
    spirit of the vagabond worked in the life of Cain in the Bible.

33. **Being driven by an unknown person** means you have
    surrendered control of your life to evil manipulators, who
    will end up diverting your destiny. Pray like this:

    > *"I unseat every evil driver in the driver's seat of my life. Let the
    > ground open up and swallow them in the name of Jesus. Holy
    > Spirit, I hand over control of every area of my life to you."*

    See? This kind of prayer brings tangible results, almost
    immediately. Prove it for yourself . . . don't just take my
    word for it!

34. **Doors closing before you enter** or something finishing
    before it gets to your turn to receive your own mean that the
    spirit of *"failure at the edge of miracles"* is working in your life.

Stopping good things from coming to you. And ushering in frustration, rejection and failure. The biblical name for this spirit is *"spirit of Pisgah"* as I've described above.

35. **Poverty**—To dream you are poor means an area of your life (not necessarily finances) has been traded out, exchanged or transferred to another. You have to recover it from the hand of evil traders and cover it with the blood of Jesus. I usually recommend a seven day prayer of recovery (with fasting).

36. **Always sitting for examinations** and not able to complete before waking up indicates obstacles on your way of progress. A spirit of failure and stagnancy is at work.

37. **Dream of death** you should rise up and begin to cancel every ordinance of death and hell against your life. And your loved ones. At times the death might just be targeted as certain areas of your life, e.g., marriage, finances, or even certain organs of the body. In any case, spiritual violence is required . . . in order to terminate the assignment of death against you.

38. **Consulting Psychics or mediums** in the dream means that evil counselors are at work against you. To divert your destiny, lead you astray and push you away from the will of God. You must also be careful of agents of the devil posing as Christians . . . on assignment to lead you astray.

39. **Having recurring nightmares** is a pointer to the fact that evil pursuers have been assigned to pursue you day and night. Once you are under hot pursuit like this, you will find yourself making costly mistakes with deadly consequences. The fact that this is recurring is a message that you have not yet given the issue the spiritual attention it deserves.

40. **Cancer** in the dream is a clear indication that there are satanic plantations that need to be uprooted from your body. And there are many ways to do this. You can pray, machine-gun style, like this:

> *"Satanic plantations in my body, be uprooted and be cast into the fire of God's judgment, in the name of Jesus."*

41. **Carrying a basket on your head** signifies the spirit of profitless hard work. That is you work like an elephant but eat like an ant. Like pouring water into a basket . . . hard work, very little result.

42. **Bats flying around** means spiritual blindness. You are not able to see things in the spirit. Therefore you are a good candidate for deception, whether in spiritual matters or in relationships. What to do?

> *Pray that the Lord should enlighten your eyes of understanding, according to Ephesians 1:17-18.*

Please note what I am saying here: If this is the only prayer you pray successfully this year, you will reap the harvest forever. I mean it. The moment the Lord opens your spiritual eyes, so many of your challenges will become a thing of the past.

43. **To see animals in your dream** generally gives you a clue to the spiritual challenges coming against you. My advice is you look closely at the characteristics of such animals in the physical and you'll have a pretty good idea what's going on in the spirit. For instance, serpents mean you are under attack by wickedly intelligent spirits, highly poisonous with an agenda to steal, to kill and to destroy. Dogs represent sexual demons and if they bite you in the dream, they will introduce the demons of lust and sexual perversion into your life. Have you ever heard some Christians who fall into fornication at the drop of a hat, saying they don't know what got into them? They are under the power of the dog.

44. **Dreams of being abandoned** means rejection, The spirit of rejection has driven many into extreme ungodliness, some in a quest for revenge, while others will do anything to gain acceptance or approval. It was this spirit of rejection that drove Cain to murder his brother Abel in the Bible. The root and consequences of rejection go very deep and you should not joke with it. You have to bind the activities of this spirit and use the blood of Jesus to erase every mark of rejection from your life.

45. **Dreams having to do with abortion** means your virtues (God-given endowments) are being withdrawn from your life. As a result of an evil cry against you in the spirit.

46. **Dreams of contacts with dead parents** mean you have ancestral covenants working against you. You have to break such covenants and release yourself from bondage in the authority and name of Jesus. If you allow those covenants to remain in place, you could find yourself developing the kind of sicknesses they had, facing their frustrations, and generally living under the supervision of family spirits that determine just how far you go in life!

47. **Dreams of being attacked by armed persons** mean a conspiracy is being hatched against your life and interests. You can abort the evil conspiracy by sending the fire of God against them. A particularly effective spiritual weapon is the *"noise of a great host"* as described in the book of 2 Kings Chapter 7.

48. **Dreams of bleeding** mean the loss of virtues, which could translate into physical losses such as the loss of a job, loved ones, finances, or even good health.

49. **Dreams of seeing cobwebs** mean hindrances designed to prevent you from fulfilling your purpose in life. You need to pray like this:

"Satanic cobwebs, be roasted by fire in the name of Jesus."

50. **Dreams of putting on earrings** mean you have been sold into slavery. Earrings are a sign of slavery in the spirit realm. You need to reject it aggressively.

51. **Dreams of wearing wigs** mean false or counterfeit glory. Stop and examine everything you are currently engaged in. Anything that does not bring glory to God should be eliminated immediately. Reject every spirit of false glory and pray for your divine original to come forth.

52. **Dreams of being handcuffed** mean spiritual captivity, and it could translate into the physical where you find yourself in a situation that is extremely difficult to extricate yourself from.

53. **Dreams of being at a funeral** whether it is your funeral or someone else's mean the spirit of death is pursuing you. You have to stand against this one with all the weapons of warfare that you know. Release the fire of God on the funeral service, disband and scatter them. Decree that you shall not die but live to declare the works of the Lord, as written in Psalm 118 verse 17.

54. **Dreams of appearing before great mountains** mean great difficulties are ahead . . . such difficulties that can melt your heart and courage and make you want to throw in the towel and quit. If you decide to deal with this, you can cut it short before it has a chance to manifest.

55. **Dreams of climbing with difficulty** same as above.

56. **Dreams of being accused in court** mean you are being cursed. Cancel, reject and revoke the curse in the name of Jesus, and replace them with the blessings of God in Deut. 28, from verse one to fourteen.

57. **Dreams of seeing padlocks** mean your destiny has been locked up. It will manifest as lack of progress, living a life of struggles and hard bondage . . . until you learn the type of prayers that break satanic padlocks like this:

> *"Every satanic padlock working against my destiny, break, break, break, in the mighty name of Jesus. I use the key of David to open all locked doors in the name of Jesus."*

58. **Dreams of wearing tattered cloths** mean poverty, shame and disgrace has been programmed into the life of that person in the spirit. Pray as I instructed against the spirit of poverty above.

59. **Dreams of eating** means that your spirit man is very dull and weak, and is not strong enough to withstand satanic activities against you. In fact, they could even feed you with human flesh and blood in the dream this way, and by the time you wake up, you find yourself physically ill. This is a popular method of planting sickness and incurable diseases in the lives of people. Jesus said: *"While men slept, the enemy cam and sowed tares."*

The tares include spiritual poison in the dream through food. You will need to vomit the evil consumption . . . and then lash out with holy anger against evil night caterers like this:

> *"You evil caterers feeding me in the dream, I command you to eat your own flesh and drink your own blood in the name of Jesus."*

This is an advanced warfare prayer that has its basis in the Scripture, in case you are wondering. In the book of Isaiah Chapter 49 verses 25-26. You now see how certain Scriptures that are not taught a lot these days could hold the key to your victory and deliverance from bad dreams, among other things.

60. **Dreams of cooking for hours on end** mean that you are engaged in unprofitable or fruitless hard work. Terminate the evil assignment by the blood of Jesus, and ask the Holy Spirit to redirect your handwork.

61. **Dreams of vehicle breaking down while traveling** means hindrances and blockages targeted against your wheels of progress. Ask the heavenly engineers to fix your vehicle and remove every hindrance on your way of progress.

62. **Dreams of entering vehicles or aircraft** and not knowing the destination means the spirit of the vagabond, that wondering spirit I described earlier, is at work again. There's an old saying that a "rolling stone gathers no moss." Recent statistics say that every year about 60 percent of people in big cities in North America move from place to place seeking greener pastures. So you end up living in a world of strangers where you barely know your neighbors next door. It is the work of this spirit. And you can pray like this:

> *"You vagabond spirits, my life is not your candidate, loose your hold upon my destiny in the name of Jesus."*

63. **Dreams of darkness of any form** signify the presence of evil powers. They cast a spiritual blanket in an environment and if you are operating there, it will seem like your heaven has become brass. You simply command the evil blanket to be roasted in Jesus' name.

64. **Dreams of being shot** mean you have satanic hunters firing arrows into your life. Sooner or later it will manifest in the physical, unless you know how to deal with it. I remember a pastor friend of mine who was shot in the dream just below the right kneecap. He woke up to see blood dripping from the wound in the physical. Soon after that he began to develop liver problems and died a few months later!

41

65. **Dreams of being naked** mean the enemy wants to disgrace you, period. The Scripture to apply here is in Isaiah 61 verse 7.

66. **Dreams of seeing yourself in chains** signify slavery either in a particular area of your life or in a total way.

67. **Dreams of having your things stolen** mean significant loss of your goods or property. Here's what you do: Blow the trumpet in the spirit to summon the spirits in charge of this operation. Command them to return what they stole seven fold in the name of Jesus. After that, release the fire of God to consume them. Cover yourself and your possessions with the blood of Jesus.

68. **Dreams of having your wedding dress stolen** is advanced warning that the spirits of marriage destruction are working against you. You need to rise up aggressively and cancel their assignment as I earlier on described. Then go on the offensive by summoning them together and releasing the judgment of the Lord against them. The Bible says: *"What God has joined together, let not man put asunder."*

So far as you were married according to biblical principles, you can stand on this Scripture to release all kinds of weapons from God's armory against them.

69. **Dreams where your Bible is stolen** mean someone is trying to withdraw your spiritual power and cause your love for Jesus to run cold. It could even lead to backsliding and ultimately, destruction.

70. **Dreams of getting confused** mean arrows of confusion have been fired against you. Return the arrows like this:

> *"Every arrow of confusion, go back to your senders in the name of Jesus."*

71. **Dreams of having your cloth torn** means judgment has been passed against you in the spirit realm. This is a very serious matter. You need to address it, canceling and nullifying it with the power in the blood of Jesus (if you are truly saved).

72. **Dreams of wandering** same as the explanation about vagabond spirit above.

73. **Dreams of being cursed** mean a satanic embargo has been placed on your progress in life. Unless you break the curse and cancel its evil consequences, you might just find life suddenly becoming a HUGE burden, friends turning to enemies, those who should help refusing to help, and misfortune dogging your every step.

74. **Dreams of having sex regularly** mean you have a spirit spouse who will do everything in its power to destroy your earthly marriage, just to keep you for themselves. They sometimes cause business failure, get anyone who comes close fired from work, and even arrange fatal accidents to eliminate all competition. People who have sex in the dream are "loaded" with all knids of spiritual materials like serpents circulating in their body without their knowledge, unexplainable health problems, and routine failure and frustration. They find it really difficult to have conception and give birth. Many of them end up being barren . . . and running from place to place for solutions. If they manage to get married, they find that the finances of the family disappears suddenly and mysteriously.

75. **Dreams of being amputated** mean significant and permanent loss, resulting in deep feelings of frustration, powerlessness and helplessness.

76. **Dreams of going back to childhood days** mean retardation, backward progress and stagnancy.

43

77. **Dreams of nursing or breastfeeding a strange baby**
mean your virtues are being spiritually withdrawn. You need
to release the fire of God to burn the strange baby to ashes.
Then you withdraw your virtues from the evil storehouse.

78. **Dream of losing your shoes** is a sign of marital failure
looming in the horizon. Better cancel it quickly and go on the
offensive to recover your marriage from the hands of evil
spiritual consultants.

79. **Dreams of fire destroying your property** mean significant loss of goods have been programmed into your future.
Pray the de-programming prayers at the end of this book.

80. **Dreams of losing your key** signify a loss of spiritual authority and power. As soon as this happens, the enemy will sharpen
his arrows and begin to fire them into your finances, marriage,
ministry, health, etc. Ask the Lord to send His ministering
angels to recover your key and to scatter every evil gathering
against your life.

81. **Dreams of dogs attacking you** mean sexual demons have
been programmed into your life. You'll have to pray hard
not to fall into sexual sins.

82. **Dreams of being attacked by cats** mean you are laboring
under witchcraft attacks.

83. **Dreams of serpents** mean you are under attack by wickedly
intelligent enemies on a mission to steal, to kill and to
destroy. See explanation above.

84. **Dreams of crocodile** mean you have strong links with
terrible spirits living in the water kingdom. It's either you
have been initiated into their evil group or you have been
donated to them as their meat, a helpless victim. These are
proud and ruthless spirits that never release their victims
unless confronted by superior firepower. By that I mean a
combined offensive using the name of Jesus, blood of Jesus,

fire, lightening and thunder of God, etc. This is a hot theater of battle reserved for veteran prayer eagles. If you find yourself confronted by this thing in the dream, my advice is to seek help urgently.

85. **Dreams of drinking alcohol** introduce confusion into the life of a person.

86. **Dreams of being exhausted always** signify spiritual sluggishness. What is known as the "snail anointing." It makes people to miss their divine opportunities, and leaves them operating in the tail region, instead of the head. This one calls for prayer and fasting, to help you renew your strength.

87. **If you find yourself vomiting in the dream** could signify an ejection of evil spiritual materials from your body.

88. **If you find yourself with rotten fruits** or eggs in the dream you need to rise up and pray against devourers, emptiers and wasters on assignment to destroy the works of your hands.

89. **If you find yourself in the midst of people wearing uniforms**, especially black regalia, it's probably that you come from a long line of occult people and your entire bloodline has been covenanted to deities you know nothing about. In the spirit realm, ignorance is no excuse. Whether you know it or not, this is still legally binding on you and generations yet unborn . . . unless you rise up now and cut off the evil flow by the power in the blood of Jesus. Please don't make the mistake of thinking that once you got "born again" these things will not affect you any more. You need to determinedly use the Word of God and prayer persistently until you have a knowing that every thread of that evil covenant has been cut off. That is when you will begin to enjoy your Christian life.

90. **If you constantly see slow moving animals in the dream,** it means you are operating with the tortoise and snail anointing. Sluggish progress or none at all; operating at the tail position instead of the head, and having the painful experience of watching others share testimonies while good things never seem to happen in your life.

91. **Seeing a multitude of flies** in the dream mean the witch-craft devourers have been programmed against your source of income and sustenance. Stand against them in the name of the Lord and release the fire of God to burn them to ashes.

Visit Our New Dream Blog

We recently set up a new blog for our website visitors to post their dreams. There are over 2,700 new dreams posted from 117 countries . . . every month. In Volume II of this manual, there will be an analysis of hundreds more of these dreams.

CHAPTER TEN

WAKE UP TO YOUR DREAM

*a*nyone having bad and ugly dreams will continue to suffer unnecessarily, if they remain ignorant of what they need to do to effect changes in the spiritual. In the last two months, I have received thousands of cases of very terrible dream attacks from my subscribers worldwide. This is a universal problem, not limited to any one culture. As I cannot answer all these emails one by one, I have explained some of the most common ones here.

Why Are Christians Still Having These Dreams?

The main reason is that most modern day Christians are not very serious with their spiritual life. Why do I say this? They are playing with sin.

One well-known man of God almost had a heart attack recently at the annual convention of all his pastors and church workers. Membership in his church are in the millions. As he was preaching, he received a message from the LORD that many in attendance were sinning and needed to repent that day. Many of them that sinned had committed such gross acts as fornication or adultery. The message he received instructed him to do an altar call and have all the culprits come forward and confess their sins. If they didn't, they would face untimely deaths in seven days!

You should have seen the stampede. Many well-respected pastors were jumping over the chairs in their haste to make it to the altar. But none of them moved initially until they heard they would die in a few days.

Needless to say, the preacher broke down and cried!

This pitiful story presents the truth about one thing. People will not do what they are supposed to do until their lives are threatened, then they act. If you are in a Bible-believing church where they preach holiness and transformation of lives, but you still refuse to change, then that makes you a good candidate for evil arrows that manifest as the kind of bad dreams we just examined.

Anyone living in any known sin has already given a blank check to dream attackers to run riot in their dreams.

I don't want you to remain in ignorance. That's why I wrote this book. If you dismiss satanic dreams with a wave of the hand thinking they are harmless, you are only deciding to allow the devil to continue to torment your life.

48   In that case, you shouldn't blame God or anyone else for your plight.

You will be doing yourself and your loved ones a world of good if you take a decision to pray against satanic dreams whenever they rear their ugly head.

Here's my advice to you:

When you are attacked in the dream, **DON'T BE AFRAID**.

You will have to learn to be methodical in dealing with these ugly dreams. If you are a child of God, you should NOT be experiencing this type of thing. But if you've had them as a result of ignorance, carelessness or prayerlessness, you can experience total victory starting NOW.

You may ask, "But I have had these types of dream for so many years without doing anything about it. Can I still take action now to effect a change and stop these dreams from recurring?"

The answer is: YES, you can!

Here's the big secret:

You can rewind your dream experiences back to your childhood days through prayer. That means you can counter the effect of all the bad dreams you had for the past ten, twenty, forty years, etc.

Here's how you pray:

> *Father, in the name of Jesus, I reverse the effect of the negative dreams I had ten years ago. Any negative consequence should be completely cancelled by the blood of Jesus. In Jesus' name. Amen.*

It is a simple prayer but it is also very powerful and it works fast, especially when you pray it like a soldier in fighting mode.

If there are dreams you have forgotten, you can ask the LORD to help you remember them. Then you can pray for the removal of whatever has caused that dream to occur. You'll be surprised that you'll suddenly remember dreams you had when you were 7, or 21, or 30. After recalling the dream, go ahead and cancel their negative impact upon your life.

In the next chapter, you'll be entering an intense practical session with real-life prayers to deal with nightmares and bad dreams.

How to Counter Dream Attacks

If you are determined to counter any dream attacks you had in the past or are having now, you need to take action right away to reverse this trend.

The Bible says in James 1:22, *"However, become doers of the word, and not hearers only, deceiving yourselves with false reasoning."*

There is no way for you to benefit from the content of this manual without carrying out the following instructions.

You can look at your life now and if you have not reached where you should be on a spiritual level, you could declare and say to Satan, *"Enough is enough. No more of you controlling my life or my dreams."* You can declare that you are completely fed up and done with satanic manipulation through your dreams. And you demand an immediate release!

You can **ONLY** do this effectively by taking the following steps:

Step 1

If you have not done so already (or if you are not sure), you must give your life to Jesus Christ and experience the new birth. When you genuinely and sincerely take this step, you will experience a major shift in your life and you will feel a HUGE burden come off your shoulders.

Here is what the Bible has to say about this matter in Colossians 1:13, 14:

> *"He delivered us from the authority of the darkness and transferred us into the kingdom of the Son of his love, by means of whom we have our release by ransom, the forgiveness of our sins."*

Step 2

You must learn to pray as if you are firing a machine gun. And do purposeful fasting along with it. I explained this in detail in my book, "Passion Prayer of Jesus the Christ"—the ebook version is distributed freely worldwide. You can download your copy from the following address:

http://www.firesprings.com/address

Prayer changes situations. Aggressive and focused praying can change your dream experiences. Significantly, this type of praying helps put a stop to the covert activities of the devil in your dream life.

Step 3

Get personal and practical help from mature believers. In most cases, you may need person-to-person counseling. What I call coaching or mentoring.

Many people have received the touch of God through coaching and e-mentoring sessions. You only have to look at the testimonies on our website (*http://www.firesprings.com*) to confirm that JESUS is still stretching forth His hand to save, heal and deliver to the uttermost. You may have to really search around your community to find a Christian ministry that teaches people to really pray. I don't mean the ones that talk about prayer . . . without actually doing the prayers. Those ones are all over the place. The prayer-focused ministries will however take a little digging around . . . and some detective work. It will be well worth your effort when you do find one though . . . because they can help you make rapid spiritual progress within the year.

If you wake up from a bad dream please follow the steps below:

1. Do NOT fear.

2. Ask the Holy Spirit to help replay the dream in sharp focus so you'll know how to respond.

3. Launch a counter-offensive by first canceling the dream, summoning the evil actors and dealing with them.

4. Recover what they stole from you in the name of Jesus.

5. Release all the big spiritual missiles against them as I've been teaching here (the blood of Jesus, fire of God, etc.).

6. Soak yourself and your loved ones in the blood of Jesus and pronounce the blessings of the LORD abundantly upon yourself.

7. Be prepared to do this repeatedly, if need be, for many days and nights. In other words, be ready for a sustained and persistent campaign.

Gird your loins and get ready to go into battle! We are going into prayers of release from dream attacks. If you have not done so already, I will advise that you lay a solid foundation by praying Steps 3, 4, and 5 prayers in *Prayer Cookbook for Busy People*. That should take you five days. Then you can follow up with these prayers for 7, 14, or 21 days depending on the severity of the attacks you've received in the past.

Chapter Eleven

111 Prayers Bullets to Cancel the Bad and the Ugly

Confession

> "And the Lord will deliver me from every evil work and preserve me for His heavenly kingdom. To Him be glory forever and ever. Amen."
>
> 2 Tim 4:18

(Please spend 10 minutes EACH DAY to sing passionate praises to God and worship him from the bottom of your heart . . . before you begin to pray.)

Day ONE

1. O Lord forgive me for any sin that's making me powerless in the dream in Jesus' name.

2. Father Lord I bring my dream life before you.

3. Lord, I ask that you charge my dreams with your fire in Jesus' name.

4. I break every curse issued against my dream life in the name of Jesus.

5. I break and loose myself from every dream captivity in the name of Jesus.

6. O Lord help me to draw closer to you in Jesus' name.

7. O Lord empower me to receive divine revelations in my dreams in the name of Jesus.

8. Every satanic power controlling my dream life be overthrown by fire in the name of Jesus.

9. Every evil bird programmed into my life from my place of birth, come out now and die by fire in the name of Jesus.

10. O Lord, use my dreams to show me my divine spiritual assignment in the name of Jesus.

11. O Lord, give me dreams that will add to my life in the name of Jesus.

53

12. O Lord show me visions of heaven in my dreams in the name of Jesus.

13. I silence every evil voice speaking in my dreams in the name of Jesus.

14. I paralyze every satanic appearance in my dreams in Jesus' name.

Day TWO

15. Dream attackers, eat your own flesh, drink your own blood in the name of Jesus.

16. Let my dreams become channels of divine revelations in Jesus' name.

17. Every altar of dream manipulation fashioned against my life, receive divine judgment and burn to ashes in Jesus' name.

18. Every strongman in my dreams, be arrested, be bound by hot chains and fetters of God in Jesus' name.

19. You strongman in my dreams, I release the fire of God against you, die and burn to ashes in the name of Jesus.

20. Witchcraft dreams, clear away by fire in the name of Jesus.

21. Every satanic arrow fired into my life in the dream, come out now and go back to your sender in Jesus' name.

22. Satanic animals appearing in my dreams, catch fire and burn to ashes in the name of Jesus.

23. I withdraw my soul from the cage of witchcraft in the name of Jesus.

24. I withdraw my glory from every marine coven in the waters in Jesus' name.

25. Let the weapons of warfare of my enemies turn against them in the name of Jesus.

26. I wipe off my name from every register of darkness in Jesus' name.

27. Every power mobilizing to attack my progress, be scattered by thunder and fire in the name of Jesus.

28. I refuse to be numbered among the dead; my enemies shall die in my place in the name of Jesus.

Day THREE

29. Any satanic priest ministering at any altar of darkness against my destiny, be arrested by the fire of God in Jesus' name.

30. Every satanic audience gathered to see my downfall, receive the fire of God and be scattered without remedy in Jesus' name.

31. O God arise, and disappoint the enterprise of the wicked against my life in Jesus' name.

32. Let every evil expectation concerning my life receive double disappointment in Jesus' name.

33. Every voice of darkness issuing curses against my life in the dream, be silenced by the blood of Jesus.

34. Every power drinking the milk and honey of my life through sex in the dream, vomit them now and die in the name of Jesus.

35. Every power, spirit or personality assigned to drink my blood in the dream, O God arise, feed them with their own flesh and their own blood in Jesus' name.

36. I shall not be afraid for the terror by night in the name of Jesus.

37. The pestilence that walks in darkness shall not prosper in my life in the name of Jesus.

38. O Lord, begin to recompense tribulation to those that trouble my dreams in the name of Jesus.

39. Every dream of demotion, you shall not stand neither shall you come to pass in the mighty name of Jesus.

40. Every dream of poverty, you shall not stand neither shall you come to pass in the mighty name of Jesus.

41. Every dream of stagnancy, you shall not stand neither shall you come to pass in the mighty name of Jesus.

42. Every dream of backwardness, you shall not stand neither shall you come to pass in the mighty name of Jesus.

Day FOUR

43. Satanic bullets fired against my destiny in the dream, you shall not land, go back to your sender in the name of Jesus.

44. Every demon idol programmed to fight me in the dream, you shall not locate my address, go back and destroy your sender in Jesus' name.

45. Every evil power demanding for my worship in the dream, receive the raging fire of God's judgment and be consumed in Jesus' name.

46. Evil wedding ceremony in the dream, be consumed by fire in the name of Jesus.

47. I reject, revoke and renounce every satanic marriage in the dream by the power in the blood of Jesus.

48. I declare that I am married to Jesus; let every power that attempts to drag me into evil marriages in the dream receive immediate judgment by fire in Jesus' name.

49. Every demonic wedding ring given to me in the dream, catch fire and burn to ashes in the name of Jesus.

50. Every demonic wedding certificate issued against me in the dream, catch fire and burn to ashes in the name of Jesus.

51. I withdraw every marital vow made by me in the dream by the power in the blood of Jesus.

52. I set on fire every evil wedding garment and ornament in the dream in Jesus' name.

53. Any power that has manipulated me into evil marriage in the dream, receive the judgment of fire, fall down and perish in Jesus' name.

54. Any evil power that has gained access to my sex organs in the dream, let the anger and fury of the Lord overtake and consume you by fire in the mighty name of Jesus.

55. Blood of Jesus, cleanse and purge my sex organs from evil deposits and plantations of darkness in Jesus' name.

56. Let all past defeats I have suffered in the dream be converted to victory in the name of Jesus.

Day FIVE

57. Every personality wearing the faces of my loved ones in the dream, be exposed and be disgraced by the light of God in Jesus' name.

58. I cancel every appointment with sorrow and tragedy in the dream in the name of Jesus.

59. Every satanic judgment against me in the dream, be cancelled by the blood of Jesus.

60. My vehicle of destiny shall not crash in the name of Jesus.

61. Evil consumption in the dream, be flushed out of my system by the blood of Jesus.

62. Strange children attached to my life in the dream, be roasted by fire in the name of Jesus.

63. Any covenant that I have formed with dark powers in the dream, be broken by the power in the blood of Jesus.

64. Every evil agreement in the dream, be cancelled and be rendered null and void by the power in the covenant blood of Jesus.

65. Any power laying evil claim of ownership upon my life in the dream, be consumed by the fire of the Lord in Jesus' name.

66. Strange pins, arrows and bullets fired into my life in the dream, I command you to materialize now and jump out by fire in the name of Jesus.

67. O Lord my God, rearrange my dream life to receive divine revelations from You in Jesus' name.

68. Any poison injected into my life in the dream, be drained out by the fire of God and the blood of Jesus.

69. Every unequal yoke established against my life in the dream, be broken by the anointing of the Holy Spirit in Jesus' name.

70. By the power that divided the Red Sea, O Lord separate me from evil dreams and nightmares in Jesus' name.

Day SIX

71. Let every careful siege of the enemy in my dreams be scattered by the thunder and fire of the Lord in Jesus' name.

72. O earth, O earth, O earth open up and swallow every satanic army marching against me in the dream in Jesus' name.

73. Let the sun, the moon and the stars begin to work against every satanic appearance in my dreams in the name of Jesus.

74. O Lord, with your strong and sore sword, arise and cut into pieces every leviathan in my dreams in Jesus' name.

75. O Lord, give unto me the shoes of iron and brass to trample upon the head of my enemies in the dream in Jesus' name.

76. Let the stormy winds of the Lord arise and destroy every satanic structure militating against my breakthroughs in the dream in Jesus' name.

77. Every pursuing power projecting itself into my dreams, be arrested, be cast into the consuming fire of God's judgment in Jesus' name.

78. Every spiritual assassin hunting for my life in the dream, I command your weapons to backfire against you in Jesus' name.

79. Let the angels of the Lord begin to read Scriptures of doom and destruction against every power pursuing me in the dream in Jesus' name.

80. Let my breakthroughs become too hot for the enemy to hinder in the name of Jesus.

81. O Lord, let your majestic voice thunder against every satanic opposition in my dreams in Jesus' name.

82. You powers and spirits from my father's house waging war against me in the dream, fall down and die in the name of Jesus.

83. You powers and spirits from my mothers house waging war against me in the dream, fall down and die in the name of Jesus.

84. I appoint all dream attackers to the sword, to famine and to captivity in the name of Jesus.

85. Every carefully concealed trap set up against my life, turn around and capture your owners in the name of Jesus.

86. Every power putting stumbling blocks on my way of progress, fall by your own sword in Jesus' name.

87. Whether the devil likes it or not, I shall experience full scale laughter this year in the name of Jesus.

Day SEVEN

88. I demolish every satanic limitation placed upon my progress in the name of Jesus.

89. Every garment of sorrow and tragedy, be roasted by fire in the name of Jesus.

90. Arrows of death and hell fired against my life in the dream, backfire and go back to sender in Jesus' name.

91. Arrows of insanity targeted against my head, backfire and go back to your sender now in the name of Jesus.

92. Arrows of marital distress, backfire and go back to your sender now in the name of Jesus.

93. Poverty activating arrows, backfire and go back to your sender now in the name of Jesus.

94. Demonic laws energizing evil arrows against my life, be broken now in the name of Jesus.

95. Let every evil unity against me be scattered by fire and thunder in the name of Jesus.

96. All my delayed blessings, be released unto me now in the name of Jesus.

97. All my diverted blessings, be restored unto me seven fold in the name of Jesus.

98. All my stolen blessings, be restored to me seven fold by fire in the name of Jesus.

99. Every power assigned to curse my blessings, fall down and perish in the name of Jesus.

100. All my polluted blessings, receive deliverance by fire in the name of Jesus.

101. Let the flying scroll of the Lord visit the camp of every power that has stolen my blessings in Jesus' name.

102. O Lord let your answers to these prayers come speedily in Jesus' name.

103. O Lord let your answers to these prayers manifest suddenly in Jesus' name.

104. O Lord, let sudden destruction break forth upon my enemies as a result of these prayers in Jesus' name.

105. Let miracles beget more miracles in my life in Jesus' name.

106. O Lord, cause me to experience 24-hour miracles as a result of these prayers in Jesus' name.

107. Father Lord, let turnaround breakthroughs be my portion as from today in Jesus' name.

108. I enter into my season of joy and laughter by the power of the Holy Ghost in Jesus' name.

109. Father Lord, help me to have a more intimate fellowship with you in Jesus' name.

110. O Lord, let me experience you as Jehovah Rapha in my dreams in Jesus' name.

111. Let the blood of Jesus speak peace unto my family in Jesus' name.

112. Thank you Lord for answering my prayers.

Chapter Twelve

17 Success Dreams and 40 Prayers to Manifest Them

Winning Dream Battles

There are two indisputable principles that underline most of the prayer bullets you see in this book. And they are responsible for the sometimes dramatic testimonies that our readers experience almost on a daily basis.

#1: Principle of Interruption Prayer

For many believers in this 21st century the enemy has completely taken over their dream lives, and things have already gone so bad that nothing short of an all-out, spiritual "shock and awe" attack on dream attackers . . . will ever be enough for them to see God's promises being fulfilled in their lives.

For instance, out of 166,741 emails from my subscribers in 2009, over 90 percent of them contained horror stories of dream attacks in the areas of:

○ Marriages and relationships

○ Finances

○ Health

Interruption prayers are designed to cut through the maze of frustration and confusion . . . and release the earthquake of deliverance to shatter the very foundation of age-old problems, some of which have been cleverly hidden for generations.

And what is "Interruption Prayer?"

It is a prophetic type of praying targeted at dismantling evil attacks and patterns from the roots. It can unleash terror against your attackers even in their dreams.

It brings restoration. It ushers in a season of victory and testimonies.

In the healing prayer book "*Prayer of Caleb,*" I explained how even father Abraham deployed this kind of prayer to help arrest a trend of barrenness and destruction against a pagan king who had gotten into trouble for trying to overstep the boundaries set by the Almighty.

#2: Principle of "Prayer Flanking"

First, what is *flanking*?

It is one of the most powerful spiritual principles in the Bible. It's an idea that works in every other area of life too. Especially in dream warfare

Simply stated: Instead of attacking a problem, a challenge or an enemy head to head, you go around them.

You flank them . . . from behind, from under, from above.

For example, in World War II, the French and their armies were behind the Maginot Line, a very, very tough defensive position.

So the Germans said: "We don't want to attack that. Rather let's *go around them* and attack through Belgium."

And that's what they did.

Six weeks later, the battle for France was over.

And the Germans had won.

You find the same thing happened in the Bible. Many times over. Let's look at a few case studies.

CASE STUDY 1:
David "Out-flanks" The Enemies of Israel

The Philistines were perennial enemies of Israel. The nation that produced Goliath, they made the mistake of coming against Israel during the reign of King David. First time, the Lord instructed David to go against them head to head. He did and the Philistines were soundly defeated.

But not for long.

Shortly after, the enemy regrouped and brought in fearsome reinforcements. Now this was a much tougher army. And they probably figured they had a better chance of victory this time around.

And that's when the Lord revealed to David how to "out-flank" the enemy instead of going against them head to head. This one strategy spelt total disaster for the Philistines. You can see the aftermath of the battle, as the Bible recounts it here:

> Then the Philistines went and made a raid on the Valley of Rephaim. And David inquired of God, saying, "Shall I go up against the Philistines? Will You deliver them into my hand?"
>
> The LORD said to him, "Go up, for I will deliver them into your hand."
>
> So they went up to Baal Perazim, and David defeated them there. Then David said, "God has broken through my enemies by my hand like a breakthrough of water." Therefore they called the name of that place Baal Perazim. And when they left their gods there, David gave a commandment, and they were burned with fire.
>
> Then the Philistines once again made a raid on the valley. Therefore David inquired again of God, and God said to him, "You shall not go up after them; circle around them, and come upon them in front of the mulberry trees. And it shall be, when you hear a sound of marching in the tops of the mulberry trees, then you shall go out to battle, for God has gone out before

> *you to strike the camp of the Philistines." So David did as God commanded him, and they drove back the army of the Philistines from Gibeon as far as Gezer. Then the fame of David went out into all lands, and the LORD brought the fear of him upon all nations.*
>
> *1 Chron 14:9-15:1*

No wonder David could confidently say in Ps 20:7:

> *Some trust in chariots, and some in horses: but we will remember the name of the LORD our God. They are brought down and fallen: but we are risen, and stand upright.*

CASE STUDY 2:
Balaam Deploys a Deadly Tactic Against Israel

This flanking principle we are discussing can work against the people of God too . . . if they are ignorant or careless with their spiritual lives.

As was the case here . . .

The greedy prophet Balaam was engaged by a heathen king to curse the children of Israel as they were coming out of Egypt. This king understood that once a powerful curse is placed on a person or nation, it will dramatically weaken them and open the door to defeat and destruction.

However, Balaam was sternly warned by the Lord not to curse His people.

But did he give up? No.

This is the reason I teach my prayer eagles to pray like this:

> *"Every power that has accepted evil assignments against my life, O Lord, appoint them to the sword, to famine and to captivity in Jesus' name."*

You see, Balaam refused to give up.

A relentless, stubborn pursuer, he simply changed his tactic. Since he was restrained from cursing Israel directly, he resorted to this "flanking" principle.

How? By advising his sponsors to entice Israel into committing immorality with the pagan nations around them.

This was poisonous, deadly counsel.

He knew that as soon as Israel fell into this sin trap, they would incur the anger and wrath of God . . . and their destruction would be swift.

Thus achieving spectacular results . . . without firing a single shot.

This is flanking at work. One of the reasons I preach strongly *against* sexual immorality among Christians is because I know it is . . .

**One of the most deadly weapons
that the devil has been using to out-flank believers . . .
And rob them of their divine destiny in Christ**

But how many churches do you know . . . that still call sexual immorality by its biblical names (fornication and adultery) or even bother to sound the alarm about their deadly consequences?

The Lord will help us all in Jesus' name.

CASE STUDY 3:
Satan Out-flanks Adam in The Garden

We all know the story of the fall of man in the book of Genesis Chapter 3. You have to remember that when the Lord gave His instructions about the forbidden fruit, Eve was *not* physically present at the time.

It must have been Adam's responsibility to pass on the information to her. Which I imagine he probably did (the Bible does not say this).

You have to watch carefully and notice that when the devil launched his historic attack, he didn't target the man Adam directly. Instead he went to Eve with great subtlety, knowing that she was the weak link.

If you read the story carefully, you'll realize how his question was framed to throw the victim into a state of confusion . . . before he struck with his lethal weapon of deception.

A tactic that would probably have failed if he'd gone head to head against Adam.

See, this was a masterful use of the weapon of flanking (in an evil way, for sure) and the entire human family has been the worse for it since.

There are many more examples in Scripture to illustrate this core principle. I remember Prophet Elisha using it against a huge Syrian army. Paul in the New Testament used it against his accusers.

67

Now why am I taking time to explain this in detail?

It is because you should know that the devil and his agents have successfully out-flanked most people in the dream. They come in while you are fast asleep and they plant sickness, poverty, frustration, ancestral yokes and burdens in the dream. At a time that most people are not very alert.

As you read this, the enemy has ALREADY arrested and diverted the blessings of . . .

Countless number of Christians into an evil warehouse in the spirit, by launching a vicious attack against them in the dream.

And this has left many believers scratching their heads and wondering whatever happened to those wonderful, exciting prophecies they receive year in and year out.

See this recent case:

> *"At the very beginning of the last year The Lord gave me a dream. I was at some woman retreat as the Holy Spirit would move there would always be three women who at different times were all fasting and praying. When it came to be my turn, with two other women, the Holy Spirit ministered to each of us, but He ministered three times to me. This is what He said to me: all of your requests, have I granted to you; everything you have asked of Me, I have given to you; it is yours you have it, ask more of Me!!!*
>
> *HE repeated all of this three times! I understand, the first part, because it is the Queen Esther's prayer, I have always had great success with. The 2nd part is where my faith has always been, last but definitely not least is God's awesome willingness to bless His children (by the way I was the only one who had the honor of receiving this three times. So my question to you is what is going on? It is another year now . . . this was supposed to be fulfilled last year!"*
>
> Name Withheld to protect Identity

I personally get thousands of emails like this one above from fine Christian folks all over the world . . . who have been wondering whether God even cares about them at all.

Little do they know that the devil has out-flanked them and intercepted their divine benefits in the dream realm . . . before they had a chance to get through to them.

Last year alone, I've had to rush out 17,712 prayer bullets to subscribers located in various parts of the world . . . to help them recover from dream attacks.

In many cases, the timely arrival of the prayer bullets, plus the step-by-step instructions on how to pray them, probably made the difference between life and death.

Like this telling case below:

> "Thanks for your newsletter it has really blessed me. I am from Africa when I received those prayer points from a friend. I was passing through stuff and I needed encouragement and those 40 prayer points helped me a lot to know that God can also work in my situation. To say the truth I wanted to kill myself. God bless you"
>
> Name Withheld to Protect Identity

Do you now see why it is *crucial* for ALL believers to learn to pray effectively . . . so they will be fully equipped to help others?

Believers everywhere should learn and re-learn how to pray effectively . . . against dream attacks.

You need to know that any Christian who refuses to learn how to deal with attacks launched against them from the dream realm may sooner or later become meat in the mouth of the devil.

And the enemy will continue to out-flank them, throttle and manipulate their blessings into his evil warehouse . . . for onward distribution to his agents and evil followers.

Secret of Your Place of Birth . . .

If the foundation of your life is tainted by idolatry, sexual perversion and bloodshed, then the enemy will use that to launch a vicious attack against you in the dream.

But you can soak your foundation in the blood of Jesus and then you can move forward to re-possess all that the enemy has stolen from you in the dream.

In order for you, a believer, to really fulfil your divine destiny in the limited time we have to spend on this earth, sooner or later, you will have to confront the enemy in your dreams. There is simply no getting around it.

Here's a big secret that dream attackers exploit.

Your place of birth is a powerful spiritual entity. And this is one of the reasons why you are required to state your place of birth wherever you have to fill out important documents anywhere in the world.

Unknown to most people, your place of birth houses the secret archives of your spiritual history, which can be easily accessed by dream attacker from anywhere in the world.

At these gates of where you are presently living, are what you could call "satanic immigration officers." One of their assignments is to scan the ancestral records of everyone coming into their territory, using powerful, super-advanced equipment that look like x-ray machines.

Their job is to locate the spiritual entry points or gates in the foundation of people's lives so they can ambush them and rob them of their divine benefits in the spirit—before they even have a chance to settle in!

Most of these attacks are initiated in the dream. It is easy for them to gain access to the ancient spiritual records of your father's house to find out what bills still have to be settled in the spirit.

Once they discover an entry point, that is a signal for them to go ahead and launch attacks against you to confiscate/transfer your divine benefits into their evil warehouse in the spirit.

The result will be that you keep dreaming of going back to your place of birth, or to you old school or neighbourhood where you grew up as a child.

This is the reason that many people who have left home and gone to where they believe is a land of milk and honey may not have much to show for their efforts, even after many years of struggles and hard work. The blessings are being sucked away in the dream . . .

Such people, in spite of their brilliant ideas and academic qualifications end up working like an elephant but eating like an ant, because their wages are being transferred to Pharaoh in their dreams.

See this telling case:

> *"July this year I decided to tell my family members to take off three days to fast and pray for our family. None of them finished the three days but I did. I prayed at the midnight hour and I had this dream.*
>
> *On the 3rd day of the fast, I dreamed me and my family members were in our home surrounded by water. Near our home, there is a big Indian sugar factory. I saw a huge monster come out of the factory and come inside our house. It would ask my father and mother for money saying that us and our neighbourhood were supposed to give it daily tribute. It would come both morning and evening daily and take our money.*
>
> *Until I rose up, looked at it in the eyes and declared that it had no power over us, we belonged to Jesus and it should never again step in our house let alone take our money (my family had a problem of health. We would spend a lot of money, in fact almost all of it on every one's health issues—cardiac problem of my mum, my sister's breast masses, etc). I've noticed that this health issue is laying off slowly but surely."*
>
> *Evelyn, Uganda*

Please close your eyes at this point and take these seven prayers with holy anger:

1. You coffin spirits programmed to waste my life, receive divine judgement by fire now in the name of Jesus.

2. Every deadly incantation issued against my destiny, be cancelled by the power in the blood of Jesus.

3. I break every yoke of failure in the mighty name of Jesus.

4. Thou powers at the gate of my breakthroughs, catch fire and burn to ashes in the name of Jesus.

5. You powers of my fathers' house, release me now and die in the name of Jesus (pray this one three aggressive times).

6. Any satanic entity divining against my life, O LORD, baptize them with madness in the name of Jesus.

7. You evil custodians of wealth in this land I bind you, I command you to loose my portion by fire in the mighty name of Jesus.

Praise the Lord.

If you look carefully at the testimonies on our websites, you will discover that as much as 70 percent are from believers who suddenly received breakthroughs in the area of new jobs, new businesses, finances, and freedom from debt.

This is not a coincidence, as we directly target their dream attackers in many of our shock prayer campaigns.

Beyond all that . . .

Because we realize that the quickest way to dispossess anyone of their divine benefits is to ambush them while they are asleep, we teach that you have to learn the kind of prayers that surrounds your dream life with the fire of the Holy Ghost.

Unfortunately many believers I meet totally disregard the effect of their dreams on the lives today. Instead they seem to be in a big hurry to lay claim on divine promises without taking a moment to deal with their dreams.

Those who attempt to possess their possession in this haphazard manner are beginning to realize that it does not work, in spite of what many people have led us to believe. If it appears to work at all, it does not last.

Their story: Up today, down tomorrow.

But once you begin to prevail in the area of your dreams, you will be surprised to find yourself bombarded by dreams of success, riches and victory.

What are these dreams?

—

17 Success Dreams

When you have prayed to the point of victory, you will begin to see different pictures in your dreams.

Before we discuss them, let's see a few examples from our testimony files:

He Received This Gift in the Dream

"Somewhere in August 2008 our company due to hard economy conditions in US decided to give every worker financial gift. At the same period I had a dream and saw our company issuing out letters and and asking us to leave the company property!

I did not understand it so I prayed for the meaning. I did not want to believe that the company which was dishing out monetary gift can at the same time send us away in lay-off or anything of that sort.

In the course of my prayers my dream was confirmed when after September financial crisis in the country and my company started laying off workers!

I kept on praying and survived two lay-offs last year. Everybody thought with two lay-offs it was over. But I kept on praying and fasting for 21 days, from November to December 2008 and did Esther fast as well on two occasions with Psalms 27 and 91 you gave us.

On the 31ˢᵗ December after praying to close out the year in that special 27 minutes prayer program, I dreamed and saw myself among a group of people with a man dressed in white and everybody hand was raised struggling to receive something from him.

Though I was standing at the back he still managed to find my hands from the raised hands and gave me the gift!

When everybody thought the lay-offs were over suddenly everybody in my company were giving WARN LETTERS on January 9, 2009 for possible lay-off in March, 2009.

The affected individuals were to be informed on February 2, 2009 to proceed on leave for the lay-off in March 2009!

> *Then came the February 2, 2009 and about half of the work force were layed off but to God be the glory I was among the selected few people who were chosen to stay to work!*
>
> *My manager then came to our office and shook my hands and congratulated me for being dedicated to work and that I am part of his plans so I am to remain and work! Praise God!"*
>
> *Simon, Arizona*

Next, we follow this email sequence . . . all the way from India

Email #1: Typical Success Dream

"As my email ID says I work for a huge global corporation. These emails have been very interesting. Last night I had a dream. In my dream, a high position person in my company gave me a big sum of money, to make a demand draft and then he handed me over his mobile, an instrument which recorded stuff, normally which secretary would used to record meetings, and a Camera, and asked me to keep the same for him and he was going into a meeting and did not want to be disturbed. He also asked me to look after a small child he had brought along. This is all I dreamt and then I was woken up by the maid in my house as it was 6:30 a.m. in the morning. I would really like to know what this means, strange dream."

J., India

Email #2: My Response

Thank you for your email. I appreciate it! Your dream is telling you that a position would be opening up soon in your company and you can get it if you want it and if you are spiritually alert. Otherwise the enemy could capture and transfer it without your knowing it. There are specific prayers you can pray to release it. Let me know if you are interested.

elisha

Email #3: Result . . . A Few Days After

"This is the most exciting thing that has happened to me. The dream in my last email has come true. I have been offered the Team Lead position in my team for a period of four months, as a test period. After this, if the management feels its working well, it will be continued, and I will get the promotion. Wonderful things are happening for me and my husband God is opening new door of opportunities . . . Thanks for your guidance"

Love and Regards, J.

So what are the dreams that will show you:

75

○ Opportunities you should be taking to usher in a new and better life for yourself and your loved ones?

○ That prosperity is on the way?

○ That you must acted immediately for best results?

○ That you must pray for your good dreams to manifest . . . quickly?

Here's 17 of them:

Seeing a garden full of fresh fruits and vegetables—This is a sign of prosperity. It means that blessings have been released for you in the spirit realm. Sooner or later it should manifest in the physical if you are alert in the spirit.

Receiving a gift or a brand new bag—If you find yourself with a beautiful brand new bag, it is a sign that you are about to be singled out for blessings. A new season of progress and favour is on the horizon.

Rainbow in the sky—A sign of God's covenant with you. This is meant to remind you of the covenant promises of God and to encourage you to step forward and lay claim on them. Now is the time to dig into the Scriptures and see what the Lord has really promised as part of His everlasting covenant, and begin to appropriate them for your life.

Being given a sword—A symbol of spiritual power and authority. With this sword you can inflict serious damage in the camp of the enemy. As you use it in prayer warfare, your victory is virtually assured.

Being given a Bible—Just like the sword above, it is a symbol of spiritual victory and authority. Your words will begin to carry divine power. When you make prophetic pronouncements, they will no longer be mere words that can be resisted. Your enemies will feel the full weight and power in the Word of the Lord spoken from your mouth.

Travelling smoothly in a car—Signifies joy and comfort, especially in business transactions that you are currently engaged in.

Bottle of honey—A powerful symbol of riches and happiness.

Keys in the dream—New openings, prosperity and breakthroughs. You will need to use these keys in prayer to open locked locked doors, and provoke a rainfall of blessings upon your life.

Speaking in tongues in the dream—Signifies spiritual blessings, purity and right-standing with the Lord. You will notice this to have an impact on your enemies. If they launch an attack against you while you are speaking in tongues, it can be devastating to their camp.

Climbing a staircase or mountain to the top successfully—This is a sign that you have overcome the barriers placed on your path of progress, and have achieved victory.

Seeing a bright shining light—This is a message to let you know that your glory is about to shine.

Being congratulated with smiles—Shows there is great success and cause for celebration just around the corner.

Seeing horses in the dream—Signifies long life and peace of mind. At this stage you should be proclaiming the Scriptures relating to long life, peace and prosperity.

Seeing a church choir singing or playing—This symbolizes a wide open door for breakthroughs for you.

Green leaves—Signify a new beginning and healing in the spirit.

Singing songs of praise—A sign of prosperity and breakthroughs, spiritually and physically.

Picking ripe and edible fruits—It is harvest time for you in the spirit; your blessings are now ripe for harvesting.

These are just some of the pictures that the Lord will be showing you in the dream, to alert you to the fact that your season of blessings is at hand.

It is at such times that you should intensify your prayers. You do not want the enemy to abort or divert the blessings at this stage. So how should you be praying?

40 Prayers to Manifest Your Success Dreams

Start with praise and worship (10 minutes)

Make this confession:

> *FATHER, I thank you for this prayer program. Thank you because the weapons of my warfare are not carnal but are mighty to the pulling down of satanic strongholds. As I go into prayer, I pray that you will manifest your presence in my life.*
>
> *I declare that JESUS is Lord over my life—spirit, soul and body. I am sanctified by the blood of Jesus. I am redeemed by the blood of Jesus. I am justified by the blood of Jesus. I have the life of God in me.*
>
> *Today, every word that I shall speak will please the Lord and glorify His name. These same words shall wreck destruction and havoc in the camp of the enemy in Jesus' name.*
>
> *I decree civil war among demons, spirits, personalities and powers set up to oppose these prayers and I break their backbone by the power in the blood of Jesus.*

77

Right now let the angel of truth begin to read Scriptures and torment every lying demon in Jesus' name. Let the bonfire of the Holy Ghost begin to burn even as I invite the Holy Spirit and hand over my battles to the LORD in Jesus' name.

Father, I pray that you will release 12 legions of warrior angels to assist me in this battle. Let your angelic host bind and restrain every demonic resistance. Let them intimidate and weaken every satanic opposition.

LORD, I pray that you will dispatch special angels of battle to evacuate stubborn spirits and their agents to the land of the wicked for mass destruction by divine earthquake, thunder and brimstone in Jesus' mighty name.

I shall possess my possessions. Let 12 legions of angels of restoration go forth into the land of the living and of the dead to recover every blessing I have lost in the past in Jesus' name.

Today, let the angels of favor be released to help me in Jesus' name. Let the angels of prosperity be dispatched to bring prosperity and abundance to me in the mighty name of Jesus Christ. Amen.

Then pray the following prayers:

1. I will arise and rise, even as my enemies continue to fall and fail in the name of Jesus.

2. Thou power that speaks success and favor, arise and speak on my behalf in the name of Jesus.

3. O Lord, let your handwriting of excellence be visible across my forehead in the name of Jesus.

4. I reject incomplete victory, I claim full term breakthroughs in Jesus' name.

5. O Lord baptize the camp of my enemies with confusion in Jesus' name.

6. My enemies shall not be able to agree concerning my case in the name of Jesus.

7. I claim the Spirit of favor in my going out and coming in by the power in the blood of Jesus.

8. Every spirit of poverty, I bind you and cast you into hell in Jesus' name.

9. Thou power that raised Lazarus from the dead, lift up my finances from every spiritual graveyard in Jesus' name.

10. Thou power that raised Lazarus from the dead, lift up my marriage from the valley of destruction in the name of Jesus.

11. Thou power that raised Lazarus from the dead, resurrect all my buried potentials by fire in the name of Jesus.

12. Thou power that raised Lazarus from the dead, ignite my prayer life by fire in the name of Jesus.

13. Thou power that raised Lazarus from the dead, inflame my heart with the love of Jesus.

14. O Lord, help me to live and breathe the fire of holiness from now onwards in Jesus' name.

15. Any power assigned to pursue me in the dream, I break your backbone with the hammer of God in Jesus' name.

16. Let the power of God catapult my spiritual life from the valley to the mountaintop in Jesus' name.

17. The power that destroyed goliath shall disgrace all my goliaths, pharaohs and herods in the mighty name of Jesus.

18. Every spiritual age-group limiting my progress in life, receive the sulphur, brimstone, fire of God, crash and burn to ashes in Jesus' name.

19. Anointing that breaks the yoke, break every satanic limitation placed upon my progress in life in Jesus' name.

20. I clear the pipeline of my breakthroughs with the blood of Jesus.

21. Thank you Lord for ushering me into a new season of joy and gladness in Jesus' name.

22. O Lord let your answers to these prayers come speedily in Jesus' name.

23. O Lord let your answers to these prayers manifest suddenly in Jesus' name.

24. O Lord, let sudden destruction break forth upon my enemies as a result of these prayers in Jesus' name.

25. Let miracles beget more miracles in my life in Jesus' name.

26. O Lord, cause me to experience 24-hour miracles as a result of these prayers in Jesus' name.

27. Father Lord, let turnaround breakthroughs be my portion as from today in Jesus' name.

28. I enter into my season of joy and laughter by the power of the Holy Ghost in Jesus' name.

29. Father Lord, help me to have a more intimate fellowship with you in Jesus' name.

30. O Lord, let me experience you as Jehovah Rapha in my dreams in Jesus' name.

31. Let the blood of Jesus speak peace unto my family in Jesus' name.

32. Every personality assigned to steal my blessings die in the name of Jesus.

33. I bring the divine executioner of God against every satanic counterattack in Jesus' name.

34. Every power and spirit of the occult released against my life, turn and face your owner and destroy them in the name of Jesus.

35. I refuse to fail at the edge of my breakthroughs in the name of Jesus.

36. O God of signs and wonders, arise and show my enemies that you are my God.

37. I refuse to bow to any satanic intimidation in Jesus' name.

81

38. I hold the blood of Jesus as evidence against any evil force unleashed against my life in Jesus' name.

39. Thou dream robbers, release my portion, receive divine judgement and die by fire in the mighty name of Jesus Christ.

LORD I thank you for answering my prayers.

*A*ppendix

Dream Diary

Remember Your Dreams

	Date	Dream	Meaning	Prayer
JANUARY				
Week 1				
Week 2				
Week 3				
Week 4				

	Date	Dream	Meaning	Prayer
FEBRUARY				
Week 1				
Week 2				
Week 3				
Week 4				
MARCH				
Week 1				
Week 2				
Week 3				
Week 4				

	Date	Dream	Meaning	Prayer
APRIL				
Week 1				
Week 2				
Week 3				
Week 4				
MAY				
Week 1				
Week 2				
Week 3				
Week 4				

	Date	Dream	Meaning	Prayer
JUNE				
Week 1				
Week 2				
Week 3				
Week 4				
JULY				
Week 1				
Week 2				
Week 3				
Week 4				

	Date	Dream	Meaning	Prayer
AUGUST				
Week 1				
Week 2				
Week 3				
Week 4				
SEPTEMBER				
Week 1				
Week 2				
Week 3				
Week 4				

	Date	Dream	Meaning	Prayer
OCTOBER				
Week 1				
Week 2				
Week 3				
Week 4				
NOVEMBER				
Week 1				
Week 2				
Week 3				
Week 4				

	Date	Dream	Meaning	Prayer
DECEMBER				
Week 1				
Week 2				
Week 3				
Week 4				